# I'D RATHER BE IN DENVER

## Dale Tooley's Own Story

COLORADO LEGAL PUBLISHING COMPANY, INC.
DENVER, COLORADO

International Standard Book Number 0-936381-00-0
Library of Congress Catalog Card Number 85-73383

To My Best Friends:
Mary Ann, my wife
and
Patrick, Keith, Brian and Kyla,
my children

# I

# THE FIRST TWENTY-FIVE YEARS

Cliff and Jo Tooley, and a peeking Dale, in East Denver, 1937.

In left photo, Dale with older brother Jack are shown in front of family log house in Fairplay, Colo., in 1935. At right, Mary Ann adjusts the mortar board at Dale's graduation ceremony at University of Colorado.

Mary Ann and Dale, on their wedding day in 1956.

## Chapter 1

# Growing Up in Denver in the 30's and 40's

*My brother, Dale, and I shared a lot in the 18 years of our childhood. We shared a bedroom, toys and clothes, laughs and experiences—and two caring, committed parents.*

*One of Dale's lifelong characteristics was apparent for as long as I can remember—his competitive spirit.*

*One hot summer day Dale, a couple of our pals and I got into a water fight. It started with water pistols, advanced to wet towels and buckets of water and then to garden hoses. The end came when Dale charged from the front of the house toward the back,* **through** *the living room, hose streaming and Mother screaming.*

*One of Dale's great disappointments was his first bike. In 1944 new bikes had gone to war. Dad found a beat-up, used one which he reconditioned as best he could. But there was no disguising that old clunker. Getting everyone up early on Christmas morning, Dale rushed into the living room to see the "new" bike he knew would be there. His fallen face said it all. It may have slowed him down, but it didn't stop him. We had our first bike race that same morning.*

— **Jack W. Tooley**

My mother's mother married my father's father, and I flunked morning kindergarten. (My mother defensively claimed that I just started school too young.) To top it off, I was born in an apartment above a garage on an alley in North Denver, and we lived in eleven different houses before I was eight years old. Despite all that, it was a great and loving family into which to be born and raised.

My parents were teenagers both when they married and when they became step-brother and sister. Mom was an enthusiastic, energetic, five-foot one blond; Dad was a hard-working meat cutter. We moved often in order to be near the butcher shops where he worked, because the 30's were hard financial times in America and in Colorado.

In the mid-30's, I can remember taking a milk bottle to the store with the few coins in it necessary to get a new bottle. The coins broke the bottle and were lost in the weeds. It was a mini-tragedy when we couldn't find the coins. We went without the milk. Firehouse gifts at Christmas were not uncommon and I even became a member of the Wyman "mice"—an auxiliary to the unemployed teenagers who hung around Wyman School in east Denver, known as the Wyman Rats. Despite those times, we didn't know we were poor, or at least if we did, we knew that everyone else was in the same boat.

Kindergarten was a traumatic experience. The teacher was Mrs. Berry. I somehow became fascinated with the drums, but because I was very "active," I was seldom good enough to get to use them. After a tumultuous semester, I was sent home with a note pinned on me stating, "Dale is not ready for afternoon kindergarten." Even at that age, this was a tough blow to handle, because all of my friends progressed while I would crawl past the school in the afternoons on the way to Simpson's grocery store, so that I would not be seen by my peers as the neighborhood "dropout." Either things looked up after that, or else Mrs. Berry could handle me no longer, and I thereafter progressed on schedule—as a mid-term student.

My older brother, Jack, three years my senior, was always good to me, except when he hit me. Actually, compared to him I often looked pretty good. When I was very young (before I can remember), in the midst of the Great Depression we lived in Alma and Fairplay in Park County, Colorado. There, Jack established a reputation of almost burning down the town and chipping the marbles out of the statue of Prunes, the burro who was memorialized for saving many miners' lives.

Medicine in those times was often catch as catch can. Rarely did we see the doctor, only twice I can recall in those early years: once when I fell off an ash pit and broke my arm in two places, and later when I had my tonsils out on an out-patient basis (delighted, because we were given ice cream when we got home). On those rare occasions when Dad would cut himself at the meat market so badly that stitches were required, I remember his removing the stitches himself to save the cost of a visit to the doctor. We were, nonetheless, very healthy overall.

About one year before World War II began, we moved into our first home which was not a rental. It was a large house (to us) on the corner of South Downing Street and East Iowa Avenue in Denver. It was in that neighborhood I learned that you always had to fight every kid on the block, so that everyone knew where one stood in the pecking order. I developed a specialty of climbing trees, once crashing down from the heights of a large willow and landing (fortunately for me) on my brother Jack. I screamed and got the attention. He didn't and had the pain.

We also became expert at digging caves. That developed into caves with rock and dirt clod fights, which in turn escalated into BB gun fights. All that ended when Lyle Graham on our block lost an eye in a BB gun fight involving kids from another neighborhood. It was not that we were unsupervised; it's just that we were innovative.

It was about the time World War II started that I had my first and only run-in with the law—at the age of eight years. Two of us were turning over park benches at Platte Park, in order to make rafts emulating those of the American marines in the South Pacific. Suddenly, the long arm of the park superintendent grabbed me and I was esconced in the livingroom of the superintendent's home at the park. He said to me, "I'll bet you're the same kid who has been chopping our hoses into one-foot lengths with a hatchet." Having recently seen a James Cagney crime movie, I replied with a line from that film, "You can't pin that on me."

At that point, the police were called and I was driven to the South Denver Police Station where my co-conspirator and I were lectured by the police sergeant. My parents had to pick me up from the police station. I complained, "If you hadn't come, I would have gotten a ride home in the police car." A proper spanking followed, but I was never again arrested and from that experience I developed a deep respect for the power of law enforcement.

World War II came with the bombing of Pearl Harbor on December 7, 1941. The next day, not knowing the true meaning of what had happened, my friends and I wrote all over the sidewalks in south Denver, "Kick Japan in the frying pan" and "Kill Tojo" (the prominent Japanese general). Quickly thereafter began a series of tin can drives, waste paper drives, rubber tire drives, practice air raids at school, and even drives to collect and contribute any knife with a blade of more than four inches.

Dad was exempt from the military service on a health basis, although he is at 75 the healthiest specimen I know.

War didn't touch us much, until the neighbor behind us was killed in a typhoon which sank his ship off the Philippines just before a naval engagement. It was then that I realized that war really does kill people, people you know, people like our young neighbor Zimmerman. Dad would often bring servicemen home for lunch or dinner. Our family was patriotic and committed to the war effort, as was everyone we knew. Finally, when World War II ended, there was great shouting and horn-honking and Dad fired his 20-gauge shotgun, which was the most memorable event of V-J Day.

During the war years, supplies were scarce, even with Dad by then owning a grocery store at 900 South Pearl Street in Denver. Our white stucco house needed painting, so one day Dad found buckets of white chalk abandoned near the Platte River. He brought it home, carefully mixed it, and we spent many days painting the house. It was a brilliant white—until the first rain, when it all ran off. It was worth a try.

A lot of home repairs took a different twist. Dad, Jack and I (and by then with a little encouragement from Day, my younger brother born in May of 1941) cemented the dirt basement of our house. As the final cement was mixed and poured, Dad tapped the concrete forms with a shovel, announcing, "Damn fine job." The tap brought all the forms crashing down, and we had twice as much work to do removing the sea of wet concrete that suddenly filled the basement.

That was the same basement where Dad decided to save money by running a series of water pipes through our coal furnace, providing "instant hot water." It worked great until a lump of coal broke the pipes—and the instant hot water system.

After Day was born, Mom and Dad decided we needed more

room, so Dad embarked on a self-help program of adding a bedroom and a utility room to our house. After installing the main plumbing system himself, Mother said, "Cliff, don't you think we ought to have the plumbing inspected first before we cover it up?" "To Hell with them!" said my Dad. A couple of weeks later, all of us helped him uncover the plumbing so that the inspector could review it.

Dad's self-help did not end with the house. When he could get time, he would weld aluminum tubing in the basement of the store. His goal was to build a house trailer, although the product looked more like airplane wings. It turned out that they were too large to get out of the basement of the store, and they remained there after Dad sold the store right after the war.

Dad also installed in the store one of the first freezer lockers in Denver. We helped him install the cork. He tried almost anything, and it usually worked out better than it was planned, because there was rarely any planning.

Automobiles were another subject which consumed a lot of our family time, energy and resources. During the war, Dad bought a small English Austin. It was so small that he, Jack and I would carry it sideways into the garage to make room for our other car. The problem with it was that it didn't run well and the steering wheel was loose. One day, with Mom pushing the Austin in her Oldsmobile, the steering wheel came off the Austin. Dad waved frantically to stop. Mom thought that meant to go faster. We saved a collision with a fire hydrant only by Dad's quick thinking when he waived the Austin steering wheel out the window.

One day Dad was in the basement under the car he had jacked up, "bleeding" the brakes. Mother was in the driver's seat pumping the brakes when he yelled at her to do so. Suddenly there was a loud "clunk." Mother said, "Cliff, Cliff!" There was no answer, so with impatience, she returned upstairs to the kitchen. Half an hour later Dad staggered upstairs with a large lump on his head saying, "What happened to you? The car fell on me."

During World War II, the doctors surmised that I might have a slight case of rheumatic fever. I was then dispatched to my Aunt Nell and Uncle Claude's house in Valentine, Nebraska, for a couple of months of "rest." That was a look at small town,

America. The most exciting thing to do was to get a parking place next to the only theatre in town on Saturday night to watch the ranchers, townspeople and Indians come to town to watch one another.

As part of this same recovery program, I spent one summer at Uncle Clarence and Aunt Wilma's farm at Merna, Nebraska. That was about as eventful as watching grass grow. The chickens were mean, but I developed a way to pry them up with a sharp stick to recover the eggs. It was a chance to look at rural America and the reasons for my not becoming a farmer. The summer was not a complete loss, because I learned to play the Marine's Hymn on the piano with one finger—to this day the only musical piece I can perform on request.

During those years, Boy Scouts offered a great opportunity to become attached to the Rocky Mountains. Every child should have the experience of being lost in the mountains, and of struggling to the summit of Arapahoe Peak, only to be confronted by two little old ladies commenting in the fog, "What a glorious day it is!" One author has said that a person is particularly attached to that with which he was enchanted at age ten—and in my case that is the mountains and the excitement of the country patriotically pulling together during World War II.

During all these growing-up years, school was not without importance. My parents saw to that. Thatcher School and Grant Junior High School were good places to learn, with all the traumas of field days, fights, girls, and the other important ingredients of growing up. The only problem I had since morning kindergarten was when my fifth-grade teacher, Mrs. London, said that I should read a particular history book because one day, if I did so, I might become a radio announcer. I sat at that period in the class schedule each day with my hands folded, refusing to read the book, for fear I would become a radio announcer.

Because of the strength of the family, it would be hard to have had a more secure childhood. Discipline may not have been according to the book, but it was effective. One day, Mom took Day out onto the curb in front of our house and told him to step into busy Downing Street. He did so. She paddled him soundly, and said, "Don't you ever do that again." He never did. Despite what the child rearing experts might say, it was much more effective than nagging reminders.

## Chapter 2

# High School and College Years: 1950-57

High school in the 50's in Denver was a time of quiet in America and of carefree times. To the extent times were not carefree, it was my own doing.

It occurred to me that perhaps I should become a world famous journalist. Accordingly, I became editor of the high school newspaper, *The Confederate*. The fact that I chose another profession was just as well. One of my first editorials was about the degree of drinking of alcohol in high school—complete with a picture of a student drinking a can of glue. That subject prompted a confrontation with the school administration at the highest levels, a demand for an apology (which was not forthcoming), and enough censorship that the First Amendment was not alive and well for the rest of my one-year term as editor.

Academics were not difficult, but much more time was devoted to dating and to a group of some thirty active teenagers with whom we ran. The custom was always group or double dating, and necking, but not too much. I was born a generation too soon.

One warm spring day, eight or ten of us decided that South High School needed to be "ditched." We piled into two jalopies and drove to the mountains west of Denver where we fished, out of season, without a license, leaving our poles unattended, and keeping fish too small for the legal limit, even if we had been legal. On a similar occasion in the same area, I remember seeing two bright silver spheres high above the Continental Divide, and watched them for half an hour or so. Suddenly, they streaked off into the distance and disappeared. This was at the time of mania over flying saucers (unidentified flying objects). For fear of appearing crazy, I did not mention the incident until some years later. It was all part of high school.

Even then, elections were big. My best recollection is

losing the election in the finals for class president, but being elected to student council and even as cheerleader in a school-wide election —something I never mention. When taking a trip with Dave Smith one summer during high school to Valentine, Nebraska, and the Black Hills, we were always careful not to mention the cheerleader role as we posed to the rural girls as athletes and swingers from the big city.

On that trip, we ended up staying at a friend's cabin near the Reptile Gardens. The only problem was that two old maid spinsters were staying there that summer, also. They said, "We won't tell, if you don't"—and after a couple of devastatingly boring evenings playing canasta, we took up with a group at the Reptile Gardens which was just as radical on the other extreme. High school was a time for such adventures.

In 1952 the Korean War was still going on and I started college at the University of Colorado. My high school friend Dean Hackett and I got a room at Baker Dormitory. We soon pledged a fraternity, Phi Delta Theta, and learned that hazing, then the rage in college, was much tougher than the hazing in our high school city-wide fraternity, Tau Sigma.

After one week in "Hell," the last weekend was devoted to swats and various kinds of hazing now not permitted in college. A concluding event was being prodded (while nude) by electric cattle prods in the basement of the fraternity house, and being told to run up the stairs. We knew ahead of time that the Great Secret was that almost no one had ever been able to walk the steps at this concluding event. The trick was that with the pain, it was instinctive to run rather than to walk. I managed to walk. I can't believe there is any harm in divulging the Great Secret a third of a century later. In a few short years, the hazing largely ended and fraternities began to reform, and at last even began to accept members of minority groups.

In my first college semester, my older brother Jack was a senior. It became his role to be my second in the intramural boxing tournament. I drew as my opponent a Golden Gloves Champion. To everyone's surprise, I won the first round. The second round was clearly his. Just before the last round began, Jack dumped a full bucket of water over my head. I leaped from my stool shouting, "You idiot!" The field house crowd loved it. He thought he was doing what a second should do to revive an outclassed boxer. Later I told him I would have lost the last round anyway.

Before that, and during my freshman year, I broke up with a girl I had dated for a couple of years. I did so indelicately. One Sunday evening walking from her dorm through the pine trees on campus, I turned to her and said, "You know, I don't love you anymore." I remember that evening saying to her over a spaghetti dinner, "It's surprising to me that you're not eating your salad." That insensitive performance on my part was not intentional.

The Ugly Parties that the fraternities used to sponsor were intentional. All of the fraternity men would put one dollar in a pot, and the one with the ugliest red-headed date won the money. I refused to participate, and looking back I can still imagine the great pain that such a cruel event left in the memories of those young girls.

Throughout college, I worked as a hasher (table waiter or dishwasher) at sorority houses and boarding houses and at the fraternity house. In return, I received free meals. Without that help, even with scholarships each semester, I would not have been able to finish college.

In the summer, there was always a variety of jobs. Several summers I cut meat at a meat market at Thirtieth and Downing in Denver in the then totally Black section of Denver. We sold lots of hogs' heads, tripe, mutton and other low-cost cuts. I was never a very good meat cutter, and often came home with a bandage over my thumb where I had not only sliced the entire loaf of lunchmeat, but a final slice of myself, as well. Other jobs included selling freezers door-to-door, laying pipeline, constructing curbs and gutters, and driving a truck for an upholstery supply house.

The most meaningful part of those summer jobs was getting one. One year, I sat from 6 a.m. until 6 p.m. in the front row of the hiring hall at the Hodcarriers' and Laborers' Union in Denver. Somehow, despite being the first one there, those who arrived later and who had connections got the slips to go out on a job. After waiting all day, I cornered one of the union executives and told him that there was a crisis in my family and that I simply must have a job. I did not tell him that the crisis was me. He then gave me a slip and that started my career as a layer of pipelines in deep trenches in Southeast Denver. The following semester, for a paper in a political science course, I went to the union hall and scoured through their records, much to their dislike. I wrote a paper concluding that this union was not all that democratic and asking why the union officials' expense accounts exceeded their salaries when they almost never went out of state.

Back in school, I became an assistant to the director of admissions, a place from which to meet literally hundreds of attractive co-eds. It was only an afternoon job, but it was a great opportunity. I decided that it would be a broadening experience to date one girl from each sorority house. After completing that, the year was not over so I decided to date a different girl each week to reach a grand total of 52 different dates in one calendar year—not realizing that on the record, it simply looked as though no one would go out with me more than once. I accomplished the final date by taking a German exchange student climbing in the mountains west of Denver. It was a fitting conclusion to a dumb idea.

Experiences with sororities were to cause me considerable problems the following year. I became assistant editor of the yearbook because it paid $500 per year. My job was to write captions for all of the pictures in the yearbook. Late one Sunday evening, at the end of several hours of caption-writing, I was confronted with a picture of four less than beautiful young women of a sorority, which had been submitted as a required part of their page in the yearbook. After puzzling over the caption, I finally captioned it simply "Hardy, Bernardi, Wilson & Stander." Those were the four star halfbacks and linemen on the CU football team. I thought nothing much more about it until the yearbook came out and I received a call from the office of the President of the University.

It seemed that the young women and their parents took a dim view of my alleged humor. It was only through some very fast talking and a good bit of luck, plus the fact that I was judgment-proof and the University repudiated my actions, that a libel suit was avoided.

The other student activities did not pay as well. I was appointed the chief justice of the student court. We conducted a first and important trial that year, and acquitted several students who had taken bricks from buildings at the University. I don't recall the grounds for acquittal, but they must have been tortured. The end result was that the student court was eventually abolished. That convinced me that elections, as uncertain as they are, provided greater certainty than did appointments. The one exception was being selected president of Heart & Dagger, the senior men's honorary society. That was done by a deck of cards. Justice Byron White of the U.S. Supreme Court and I hold that same distinction of being lucky at cards in drawing that particular post.

I was urged by friends to run for student body president. I did so in a campaign which was every bit as prolonged and time-consuming as some others I would subsequently conduct. We created a platform, ran a slate of candidates, and I, and a majority of our ticket, were elected. It was a great experience in dealing with people. I began the precedent of attending the Board of Regents meetings, and to my surprise, found the board receptive both to my attendance and to appropriate participation. The same was true with the Boulder Chamber of Commerce, where there had always been a schism between the University students and the business community in the City of Boulder.

We fulfilled all of our platform, but our main contributions were to help bring a buffalo to the University of Colorado, a precedent which still exists, and helping place a hundred 1956-57 Hungarian students who fled to the United States during the Hungarian revolution against the Soviet forces.

There was one other lasting effect of the presidency, however. Late one Friday at the student government office a member of the Boulder Chamber of Commerce called to ask why the University of Colorado had not submitted any entries in the Miss Boulder contest. He said, "Who knows, there might be a future Miss America on the campus." At the last moment, I decided it was worth a call and rang up a friend at the Pi Beta Phi house.

I explained the crisis and she said, "Oh, I'll bet Marilyn Vanderbur would be willing to be a candidate. I'll ask her." That is how Marilyn Vanderbur became an entry in the Miss Boulder, then the Miss Colorado, and ultimately the winner of the Miss America contest. Occasionally, it pays to answer the phone.

After five semesters of college, I obtained special permission to enroll in law school. I was the only law student not old enough to vote in the November elections. That decision proved to be a fortuitous one, however, because it caused me to change hashing jobs. I began that fall semester hashing at Perry's boarding house next to the Flatiron Theater in Boulder. [Interestingly enough, years later all three of our sons would live on the very site of that boarding house in apartments which they managed as they, themselves, helped to work their way through college.]

The first morning I noticed that there was a brunette with tightly curled hair who seemed to be an engaging sort and clearly the best of the entire group. One thing led to another, and I met Mary Ann, whom I would marry less than two years later. She has proved to be the most remarkable woman and wife anyone could have been fortunate enough to meet while bringing her scrambled eggs.

After meeting this love of my life, I decided the best thing to do would be to impress her. Two friends and I took our dates to the ghost town of Montezuma near Argentine Pass west of Georgetown. Figuring that a thrill was important to make a good impression, we found an abandoned gold mine with a track still intact and with a mining car on it. We placed the three co-eds in the mining car and rolled them deep into the shaft. I pulled the lever on the car to see what would happen and dumped all of them into the cold water which had seeped into the mine. We did take them out for spaghetti dinner that evening, though.

The next formal date was one where I knew I had to do better. With Lyle Quinby, who was then president of the student body, and his date, Donna Darley, daughter of the president of the University, we went to the Tropics Night Club in Denver. This was a club known for its lustful performances, particularly by a 52-inch breasted woman known as "Tempest Storm." I was not yet old enough to drink, and had not admitted this to Mary Ann. After some maneuvering, we were each able to get a Tom Collins. (Mary Ann was legally of age by a few months.) The show was so gross (exciting, thought I) that Donna and Mary Ann spent most of the evening in the ladies' room. However, subsequent dates got better.

Our engagement was relatively short and we agreed to marry on June 9, 1956. Because this was a no-frills affair, we had no printed invitations, only invitations by word of mouth.

The wedding was in the livingroom of the Kappa Alpha Theta house on University Boulevard. It occurred to me the morning of the wedding that I had not renewed my draft deferment, having just recently passed the then-required draft deferment examination. Dressed in my best (and only) suit, less than half an hour before the wedding, I was negotiating my student draft deferment at the University offices while my bride was expecting me to be only a few yards away pacing the floor. Fortunately, I made it just before the ceremony began, and no one was the worse for wear, except for Mary Ann when she later learned of the events of the day.

Our honeymoon was a weekend in Colorado Springs with a side trip to the Royal Gorge. It could not have been better, and our $195 Chevrolet automobile was the joint contribution to our marriage assets.

To show you the kind of woman I married requires a couple of examples. I was elected canebearer for our graduation class (the most likely to succeed). As such, I led the ceremony and when the time came to receive the degrees, mine was blank. I thought the University was trying to tell me something. Mary Ann confidently said that there was no problem at all, that it could not have been anything I did. She proved to be right.

About a month after that graduation, I sat for the Colorado bar examination. I studied hard for it and thought I did reasonably well. However, I found it such a draining experience that I said I wouldn't take it again if I failed it. With that, I was sent off in military service to Fort Leonard Wood, Missouri.

In those days, the bar examination results were not posted nor given by private letter. Instead, on a given day they would simply appear in the newspapers. While I was blissfully in basic training, the bar examination results came out. The headlines read, "Ninety-two pass Colorado Bar Exams." Mary Ann quickly looked through the alphabetical listing and my name was not included. She had no apprehension at all about the fact that I may not have passed. She was convinced that I had done nothing wrong, that it must simply be a mix-up with the Bar examiners, just as in the case of my degree. She counted all the names. There were only ninety-one listed. There was never any doubt whatever in her mind that the unlisted name was mine.

She scurried from newspaper stand to newspaper stand until

she found an edition of the other major Denver paper, which properly listed ninety-two successful candidates, and my name was among them. She calmly wrote me a letter saying, "You passed." That kind of confidence has to help a fellow.

## Chapter 3

# The Military

My experience with the military began in Air Force ROTC at the University of Colorado. For two years, I participated in everything except the parades. I didn't participate in the parades until the very end for two reasons: First, my shoes didn't fit. Second, the hat didn't fit. Finally, an Air Force captain said that I *would* be present at the parade review in honor of a visiting general.

I miraculously found shoes that fit, but the hat didn't. I managed to stuff socks into the hat and make it at least stay above my eyebrows. Suddenly, in the course of the parade, the commander yelled, "Eyes right." My eyes snapped right, my head snapped right and the socks snapped right over my eyes. It was an embarrassing demonstration to the entire unit, I was reminded later.

After having failed the depth perception test so that I could not fly airplanes, I decided my country would be better served if I were to join the National Guard after completion of law school. That I did. In less than a month, I was on a train headed for Fort Leonard Wood, Missouri, along with a host of others. It was August and well over 100 degrees, and all I heard about was how cold it would be in the winter.

We received the usual shaved head treatment, clothes that didn't quite fit and assignment to a unit. The unit was almost all college graduates who were less than enthusiastic about military life.

One day I was assigned the duty of barracks guard. It was a memorable day. The first event was an unexpected visit to our barracks by a major. I had been reading a law book while lying on the floor, with my head propped up by my right arm. When the major appeared, I was asleep and so was my right arm. I heard him in the latrine and snapped to attention. When I tried to salute, my hand looked as though I had been squeezing oranges. The major said, "What's the matter with your hand, soldier. And don't salute me while I'm using the latrine." His report was not glowing.

That afternoon I was reminded that I certainly should heat up the boiler so that the troops would have warm water when they returned from the day's training. I decided if a little hot water was good, a lot of hot water was even better. I generated a fire which brought the water temperature to a new high. It was soon apparent that I was close to burning down the barracks. I decided to slow the fire by throwing water on it—unaware that by doing so, I would crack the furnace and the water system would produce no hot water at all. The troops returned to plenty of water, but all of it cold. That was the last time I was assigned to serve as barracks guard.

As the weeks dragged on, it became apparent that nothing important happened during the first couple of hours in the morning. Some of my companions and I acquired a large volume of pill bottles. We would place these on our foot locker when the wake-up bugle sounded. The inspectors always thought we must legitimately be on sick call with that much medicine. That always fooled the officers. It didn't fool the sergeant. He asked for our sick call slips, and we meekly confessed. We were disciplined, threatened with court martial and required to report to the day room every hour for three days. After that, we were remarkably healthy.

After completing basic training, I was assigned to the dangerous mission of clerk typist school. About that time, I learned of my having passed the Colorado bar examination, and arranged to be admitted to the bar with the oath administered by a colonel at Fort Leonard Wood. That led to my being transferred to an Army Judge Advocate General office where I gave uneven tax, estate planning and debtor's rights advice.

In the process, I learned of the Soldier's and Sailor's Civil Relief Act of 1941, and suggested to Captain Casey that this might be good grist for the required Saturday lectures to the troops. Soon, I was lecturing to movie theatres filled with hundreds of troops on their rights under that law legitimately to delay payments in some circumstances. Each day of those lectures, I was treated like an officer. Each day on returning to the barracks, I was treated like the E-2 I was, one rank below Private,

First Class.

Finally, we got a weekend leave and I was able to meet Mary Ann in Springfield, Missouri. The main claim to fame of Springfield is that there is a large federal prison there. We met and appeared to be registering at the hotel under phony names. (Although we were married, we looked guilty.) A few days of civilian status did wonders in bringing order out of the military chaos. After that it was only a short time until I was released to a reserve unit in Denver.

I began practicing law in February, 1958, but one night a week I was assigned to an artillery unit at the National Guard headquarters at 300 Logan Street. Engraved above the door of that building are the words "Builders of Better Boyhood." To this day, I have never seen an artillery piece fired, although I did see a training film once of guns being fired. Our National Guard unit did not have a remarkable record. The only time since the Korean War it was activated, was to locate a girl who was lost in the mountains. By the time the unit could be mustered and fully outfitted in the costumes of the day, the Boy Scouts found the girl.

I learned that one could become an officer by going once a month to a weekend training group at Camp George West near Golden, and by spending two weeks for two consecutive summers at Fort Carson near Colorado Springs. Given my awareness that an officer lives better than a private, I jumped at the chance. However, at that time the head of the Colorado National Guard was General Robert Charleton. He was an attorney. While I was a private and attending the OCS sessions, I happened to have a case against General Charleton. He was so proud of his title that in court the judges addressed him as General. Fortunately, they did not call me Private, but Charleton knew I was a private. I won the case, and it caused no end of embarrassment for the General.

After my hard-earned promotion to second lieutenant, I was assigned to the 124th Signal Battalion in Englewood. The other second lieutenant was the now junior U.S. Senator from Colorado, Bill Armstrong. Together, we were probably the least experienced lieutenants in the Reserves. However, most of the members of the unit were experienced in communications and worked either for the telephone company or Public Service Company. So as long as we stayed out of their way, the unit performed well.

One weekend training day we took the troops to an area in Larimer County. Bill Armstrong and I decided our best service would be to stay on the bus and discuss philosophy and politics. We spent the day debating the issue of whether children were entitled to a free public education from kindergarten through twelfth grade. At the end of the day, all the telephone poles had been erected and we returned to Denver. Later, we learned that under our supervision, or lack of it, the poles had been erected too close to the end of a runway, so we returned for yet another training day to take them all down.

Tiring of the Signal Corps, I learned of a research unit at the Federal Center in the Army Reserve. I applied to conduct a study of the risks of avalanches. Instead, I was transferred to a Judge Advocate General unit at Fitzsimons Army Hospital, where I finished my military career some six years after first leaving for Fort Leonard Wood.

Years later, I was to be one of the two invited public officials from Colorado to attend the U.S. Army War College at Carlisle Barracks, Pennsylvania. Often, the colonels and generals attending would ask, "Were you in the service?" My answer was always, "You bet I was, during the big one: the first Lebanon crisis."

That experience at the Army War College caused me to begin an effort to develop better coordination between our office and other public officials in Denver, and the commanders of the various military units in the Denver area. I developed a very real appreciation for the quality of many of those officers and a greater degree of respect for those who serve in the military than I had while I was actually in the service.

# II

# PROFESSIONAL AND FAMILY LIFE

Dale and his three sons—Patrick, Brian and Keith, 1965.

Mary Ann and Dale at home with the children, 1967.

Out for a stroll, 1972, with Kyla, Patrick, Keith and Brian.

Private Dale Tooley at
Fort Leonard Wood, Mo.,
1957.

# Chapter 4

# Law Practice Years, 1958-1972

*Dale Tooley was just about the most efficient and effective lawyer I have known. Whenever he participated in a trial or difficult negotiating session, his competence seemed to fill the room.*

*His integrity, keen sense of fairness and reassuring presence commanded tremendous respect from clients and adversaries alike, and he invariably assumed the primary leadership role in resolving whatever dispute confronted him.*

*He also could laugh at the rare mistakes that he made in the practice, and he always found time to take on more than his share of pro bono cases. The legal profession grew because of Dale, for indeed he was truly professional.*

— **Thomas G. Brown**

Within days after returning to Denver from Fort Leonard Wood, because we would rather be in Denver, I went to work as an associate with the large Seventeenth Street law firm of Dawson, Nagel, Sherman & Howard (now known as Sherman & Howard). The cases were important ones and working with John W. Low, an outstanding attorney, I received substantial courtroom experience in the year and a half I was with the firm. However, I also learned that associates were required to handle tasks for regular clients which partners would prefer not to handle. One such case involved an old gentleman named Mr. Braerton.

Mr. Braerton was in his eighties, and each day during the rush hour, he drove slowly, i.e., 15 miles per hour, down Speer Boulevard to his home in East Denver. Each day, he created a traffic jam of substantial proportion. Finally, the police cited him for being too old to drive, because he was not driving fast enough. That resulted in his demand for an examination by the Motor Vehicle Division so that his privilege of driving could be restored. I was the designated victim for the defense.

I picked up Mr. Braerton and took him to the Motor Vehicle Division at West Sixth Avenue and Bannock Street. The hearing examiner who was the designated victim for the State was Examiner McIsaac, a courageous individual. The first step was the written examination.

Mr. Braerton would be asked questions such as "How long before sunset and sunrise do you turn on your lights?" His answer: "Don't worry about me, young fellow, I always turn them on in time." Another was, "When can you turn around on an open mountain highway?" His answer: "I just don't do that, young fellow." More as a favor to me and a desire to conclude the examination than anything else, McIsaac decided to pass Mr. Braerton on the written examination. We didn't bother with the eye test.

"Get your automobile and show up at the back gate," said McIsaac. Mr. Braerton had no car, so I offered him mine, provided that I could ride in the back seat. That was agreeable. He started by revving the engine, putting the car alternately in reverse and in low gear, and causing huge billows of smoke to come from the transmission. We finally made it to the back door and McIsaac took his position in the death seat. This was before the era of seatbelts.

"Go out on Sixth Avenue and turn right," commanded McIsaac.

"You bet I will, young man," responded Mr. Braerton, as he hurdled into Sixth Avenue in the teeth of oncoming traffic, spun a sharp right and, amazingly, avoided a collision. The screeches of brakes told us we were in for a difficult test.

"Turn right on Broadway!" commanded McIsaac. "Why, I remember when this used to be a savings and loan office," mused Mr. Braerton as he turned from the right lane of Sixth Avenue onto the left lane of Broadway, crossing at least four lanes of traffic in the process. "Turn left at the next corner," said McIsaac. Braerton did so, but missed the corner, wheeled through a filling station, drove between the station and the gas pumps and miraculously came out on Fifth Avenue heading east, having missed all pedestrians, automobiles and structures. McIsaac looked at me and shuddered. I tried to keep a poker face, although I was pale.

McIsaac guided Mr. Braerton back to Sixth Avenue and Bannock, whereupon Braerton drove my car into the rear end of a police car.

The policeman seemed to take it in good grace, but more black smoke billowed out of the car as Mr. Braerton attempted to get it launched into forward gear. "How did we do?" asked Mr. Braerton. "I'll send you my decision in writing," said McIsaac diplomatically, as he pulled me aside and whispered, "He's a menace to society. We can't let him get behind the wheel again. He almost killed us." Mr. Braerton got the notice that he could no longer drive. He was satisfied that he had had a fair hearing, and he remained a good client of the firm.

Most of the work I was assigned by the firm was substantial and complicated, and I liked the lawyers. Nevertheless, when I was offered a position with the smaller, vibrant firm of Lesher, Schmidt & Van Cise, I quickly accepted it. It was a public-spirited firm. Don Lesher was a former Republican legislator. Dick Schmidt was to become General Counsel of the United States Information Agency under President Johnson and also Chief Counsel to Senator Stuart Symington's special committee investigating the grain storage scandals involving Billie Sol Estes. Ned Van Cise is now a Judge of the Colorado Court of Appeals. Charles Goldberg, a later partner, was to become a Judge of the District Court, as was Richard L. Eason. Roy Romer, then a state legislator, was later to become the Democratic candidate for United States Senator and then Colorado State Treasurer. Hugh McClearn, former Manager of Safety of the City and County of Denver and the one who would manage my last campaign for mayor, was a partner and the firm became Van Cise, Freeman, Tooley & McClearn. Until 1972, when I was elected Denver district attorney, I enjoyed a fraternal and prosperous practice with this firm.

We handled many cases, most of them civil. For several months, I was in trial every week on a different case, but there remained plenty of time for civic affairs and pro bono work. One such effort was in the hot summer of 1965, when I volunteered to be a trial attorney to try civil rights cases in Mississippi.

It was at the height of the civil rights movement. A number of people had been killed in Mississippi that summer, and the social pressures on the local bar were such that no Mississippi lawyers would handle civil rights cases, defined as representing a White from the north in a civil rights case or a Black from anywhere, whether a civil rights case or not. This was complicated by the fact that there were only two Black attorneys then admitted to the Bar of Mississippi.

I arrived one hot Saturday morning in Jackson to be confronted by headlines which said, "Niggers Riot in Watts," referring to the civil rights riots in Los Angeles. This was after the march to Selma and before Martin Luther King, Jr.'s assassination in 1968.

One of the cases I tried was the defense of a young Harvard student charged with disturbing the peace in Scott County, a notorious hotbed of discrimination in those years. My client had been invited by the Deacons of the Mt. Ludlow Zion Baptist Church to visit the church one Sunday. Because the congregation was twice as large as the church could hold, half the congregation gathered outside under the trees while the other half listened inside to the sermon of the day. My client was invited to explain to those outside, in sequence, their rights to become registered to vote, since a federal registrar was soon to be in Scott County. At that time, a constable arrived, jailed my client and charged him with disturbing the peace.

I drove to Branch, Mississippi, to try the case. It was difficult to find the courtroom because I was wearing a coat and tie and Mississippians were reluctant to speak to me, thinking I was either a reporter or an FBI agent. Finally, a woman explained that the trial would be in an abandoned store, which could be located behind three burned Ku Klux Klan crosses a short distance away.

When I arrived at the courtroom, all of the Blacks stood outside in the muggy weather, while all of the seats inside were filled by white citizens. As we prepared to try the case, the prosecutor said to me, "We've all decided to drop the charge." Congratulating myself silently on the victory, I began to pack up my briefcase. "But wait a minute," he said. "We've decided to charge your client with a more serious offense, that of disturbing religious worship."

"Wait a minute," I said to the Judge. "I have not seen the

charge and we are not prepared to try a different charge at this time. I ask for a continuance." The Judge looked at the prosecutor. The prosecutor shook his head no. And the Judge said, "Denied." We proceeded to trial.

The prosecutor addressed all white witnesses by "Mr." or "Mrs.," but addressed all black witnesses by their first names. The prosecution had no evidence of any disturbance whatever. If anything, the evidence all proved that my client was innocent. At the conclusion of the prosecution's case, I made what I thought was an eloquent and persuasive motion for judgment of acquittal. Again, the Judge looked at the prosecutor, the prosecutor shook his head, and the Judge said, "Denied. Does the defense have any evidence to present?"

One by one, I called to the stand the deacons of the church, who testified in quiet dignity. These deacons were the first Blacks to testify in a civil rights case in Scott County. Uniformly, they testified that they had been present that Sunday morning, that there was no disturbance whatever and that they had invited my client to be present and to speak to the congregation outside the church. Following closing arguments, the Judge again looked at the prosecutor, the prosecutor gave a signal and the Judge pronounced, "Guilty." I was stunned and angry as my client was handcuffed and taken to jail to begin serving a one-year sentence.

Afterwards, I talked with the prosecutor who said, "I knew you were going to lose." "How is that?" I inquired. "Well, at this level of the Mississippi judicial system, the Judge gets paid if he convicts, and he does not get paid at all if he acquits."

"That is outrageous. What about *Toomey v. Ohio,* decided almost 40 years ago, holding that such a system is unconstitutional?" His response: "Well, we don't pay much attention to the U.S. Supreme Court down here."

As I drove back to Jackson, I became increasingly angry. I first arranged to remove the case to Federal Court, and had my client released. (Ultimately, the case in Federal Court was dismissed and my client was freed without a record, but only after the scare of his life.) The broader issue remained: How in the United States could a system operate without an impartial judiciary?

I went to see an Assistant Mississippi Attorney General the next day. He said, "Look, I know you're right on the law. But you're only down here temporarily and we have to live here. Nevertheless, if you will work up all the case authority and draft a statute, I will take it up with the Supreme Court and see if we can refer it to the legislature and change this system." These were the first reform words I had heard in my two-week stint in Mississippi.

When I returned to Denver, I organized a dozen law students at the University of Colorado and we did a comprehensive job of researching the law and the cases, and of drafting a model statute. True to his word, the Assistant Attorney General got the law passed, and today at all levels of the Mississippi judiciary, judges are paid whether there is a conviction or an acquittal. The tragedy is that it took more than forty years for the U.S. Supreme Court ruling to be implemented in Mississippi.

However, years later I was to meet in Denver with Alvin Bronstein, who had headed our volunteer lawyers office in Mississippi. He reported that things had been moving forward rather well in Mississippi and that he had left to do work up North because the progress was slower there. He said that the Mississippi Bar was now handling civil rights cases, that Blacks were being admitted to the Bar regularly, and that he was hopeful that discrimination would be handled, in the long run, more effectively in the South than in cities of the North.

The experience in Mississippi was more than just an experience in a different judicial system. Part of it was an experience in violence. Young roughnecks would ride through the towns of rural Mississippi firing high powered rifles into the Freedom Houses where young civil rights volunteers lived.

Once, I tried a case in Canton, Mississippi, before the judge, who was also the head of the Klu Klux Klan in that town. It was a case involving an alleged assault with a deadly weapon. I asked a witness what he had seen, and the young Black man said, "I seen a goon." I asked the questions several times, trying to determine just what a "goon" had to do with the case. Finally, the judge called me to the bench and said quietly, "Young man, we heard the witness say he saw a gun, now ask your next question."

On another occasion, in a courthouse in rural Mississippi, I saw, and removed, an advertisement on the official courthouse bulletin board announcing that imperial wizard Robert M.

Shelton of the Klu Klux Klan would be appearing to give a speech on Friday. At the bottom of the announcement were the words "On Highway 80. Ask any law officer for directions." After that, I didn't discount those young Black civil rights workers who would report that they were charged with "resisting assault."

That decade and a half from 1958 through 1972 was a time of great social change in America, a time of diversity in the practice of law, and a time to contribute as a citizen in the causes and efforts of our time. My law partners patiently permitted all of that. When I returned to the law practice in 1983 with the outstanding firm of Welborn, Dufford, Brown & Tooley, my partners were equally patient and generous toward pro bono and civic activities.

## Chapter 5

# Growing Up With the Children

Growing up with the children began a week or two after Patrick's birth the day before the fourth of July in 1959. By August, he was fishing with us, screaming and generally being what is known as an "active" child. Before Patrick was three, he was joined by his brothers, Keith and Brian. We finally figured out what caused children, after thinking we might never have any!

It was not until years later that Mary Ann and I realized that three under three years of age meant a tremendous energy drain, particularly on her. The three of them multiplied the activity level geometrically.

Eating out at restaurants became an adventure. Once, all of the boys simultaneously dipped their faces in the spaghetti sauce at Colacci's restaurant in Louisville. It is little wonder that many of the patrons seemed to leave early. Each of the children had experiences such as Patrick's, of tipping over backwards in his chair, plate full, at the Four Seasons Restaurant in Chinatown in San Francisco. Eventually, we learned that the best way to keep them quiet was to teach them blackjack.

By 1966, Kyle (who has recently changed her name to Kyla) joined us. We had instructed Dr. Jerome Harris, the excellent doctor who delivered all of our children, to tie Mary Ann's tubes if the fourth child was a girl. In the waiting room at General Rose Memorial Hospital in Denver, Dr. Harris described to me the arrival of Kyla, and mentioned in passing that he had performed a tubal ligation. Having yet another child was traumatic enough and I didn't clearly hear him.

"You did what?" I asked. Dr. Harris became visibly pale and nervously explained that was what he thought our instructions were. Color returned to his cheeks when I said, "Oh, I understand. That's what we told you to do."

Actually, Kyla would not have been born except for help

from Adlai Stevenson, the Democratic nominee for President in 1952 and 1956. Stevenson was scheduled to speak at a Western States Democratic Conference I was to attend, but his untimely death caused a postponement of the conference—the very weekend Kyla was conceived. Some years later I told his son, then U.S. Senator Adlai Stevenson III, that our daughter's arrival was a result of his father. He stuttered, became flushed and returned to normal only when I explained the full story.

There is an old saying that a child always brings with it bread in its mouth. We found that a child always brought with it a move. When Mary Ann became pregnant with Keith, we moved from our $80-a-month rental at 2680 South Knox Court to a majestic house costing almost $15,000 at 140 Daphne Way in Broomfield. When she became pregnant with Brian, we moved up the economic notch several thousand dollars more into a home at 646 Williams Street in Denver. When Kyla was born, we moved several blocks east to our home at 635 Vine Street.

Tracing the moves and the prices of houses was a glimpse at inflation in America. Our home at 635 Vine was purchased for $33,000, and 13 years later we were to turn down an offer of eight times that amount. At one point, as the children began leaving for college, I almost persuaded Mary Ann that we should reverse the story line, and begin moving back into our previous houses as each child returned to college. It was a great idea only in theory.

It developed that all of the children began to learn to swim at the same time. It was not uncommon to see an almost drowned father scurrying from end to end of the swimming pool bailing out a child as he or she ran out of breath. Actually, their learning to swim was probably a matter of survival. They became, in the process, even more independent. Brian used to swim frantically and when anyone approached him, would yell "Whim away!"

With four active children, accidents became almost routine. One of my first memories of these accidents was arriving at the corner of East Seventh Avenue and Gilpin Street to see two of our young sons covered with sheets, after they were involved as passengers in an automobile accident—one of the few they didn't cause. They were not dead, simply resting, the driver said. They were released from the hospital without serious injury.

Brian once was struck by a car while riding his bicycle. He went into shock and kicked the lights out of a Denver policeman who was trying to help. What depressed him was being in Children's Hospital. He would only answer questions with the single word, "Yup." Kyla, being more careful, seemed to avoid such traumas, although all accidents were a matter of good spirit. We had a standing joke that when any of the children on their bicycles hit a tree, their obligation was to apologize to the tree. That irritating memory seems vivid in all of them.

One day while skiing at Loveland, in his early skiing days, Patrick tumbled in the powder snow. He said, "Dad, I hurt my leg." Being father of the year, I replied, "Come on, Patrick, get up. You're OK." When I saw he couldn't get up, I figured he had some slight sprain, so I picked him up and skied to the warming house with him. Only then did we learn that he had suffered a spiral fracture which would make him the talk of third grade at Moore School. After that, I always took their statements about injuries more seriously.

Skiing with the children was like being in combat. I remember one particularly vivid scene where one of the children dropped a ski pole and tried to recover it while the lift was still moving. He slipped and was hanging on with one arm. His brothers were struggling to keep from falling off their chair and slipping back down the access lip at the end of the lift. Except for being panicked, Mary Ann and I were regaled in laughter. They all survived and became excellent skiers, far better than their father.

Brian had a knack, whether skiing or not, of always losing his clothing. He set the record one time when, on a rather cold day at Winter Park, he skied from the top to the bottom and, in the process, arrived at the bottom without his parka. "Where's your parka, Brian?" I asked. Brian looked surprised, noticed for the first time it was missing, and said, "I don't know." The parka showed up at the bottom of the mountain at the end of the day, still a mystery as to how it came off and how it later arrived at the bottom.

It was rare to have a pair of gloves which matched, and we seemed to have always a surplus of left boots. Scarves were utterly expendable, and jackets always seemed to be on someone else. If we could ever have accurately totaled the clothing costs for the four children, we think it would equal their college education expenses.

The mountains became an important place to be together with the family. Picnics and hikes abounded, including one raft trip down the Yampa and Green Rivers in Northwest Colorado and Utah. To this day, the three boys still vividly remember our throwing them off the rafts (which was perfectly safe, because they were wearing life jackets), and playfully pouring beer over their heads as they tried to get back aboard. Kyla, on the other hand, was always a study in science in the mountains. No twig or flower, no matter how small, avoided her attention. Many short hikes with her became interminably long ones, but fascinating each step of the way.

As the children grew older, they joined in the practical joke syndrome which permeated the household. Once, while the family was climbing the Flatirons near Boulder, Mary Ann thought Patrick might have fallen from a high ledge. I fixed Patrick up with apparent crutches and a bandaged leg and covered his forehead with berry juice. That was not a particularly funny practical joke, because Mary Ann went practically into shock before she realized that this was not real. The practical jokes the children played on one another are even now only gradually surfacing as they feel the statute of limitations on their liability has begun to run.

On a number of occasions, as the great hunter, I took the children on rabbit hunting trips. Keith was particularly fond of hiding behind bushes, jumping up with his fingers where a rabbit's ears would be, and exclaiming, "Hey, Dad, here's a rabbit!" Equally unhelpful was our dog, Thunder. On one occasion near Castlewood Dam, Thunder chased a rabbit into a bramblebush, and was circling in on the frightened rabbit in ever decreasing concentric circles. One couldn't shoot without hitting Thunder (although that was a temptation). When the circle finally closed, the rabbit had long since jumped out of the brambles and Thunder was her usual frustrated self.

Thunder was a gift to one of the children for a birthday. The dog seemed bright enough, a cross between a poodle and a terrier. However, she was never able to be housebroken, so she, rather than our cars, lived year-round in our garage. It was the largest dog house in town. Through the force of our wills, we turned her attitude into that of a Saint Bernard. She did not enter our house more than half a dozen times in her long sixteen-year lifetime.

Her demise came the day after she barked one night outside of her garage. I went to the deck, made two perfect snowballs, and herded her with them as she retreated to the garage. The next day at dinner, I boasted of my marksmanship and how one silences a barking dog.

"You'll never do that again," said Brian. "What does that mean?" I asked. Only through vigorous cross-examination did I learn that the Judases of the household had decided that Thunder, who was in terrible shape by then due to her age and other infirmities, had to be put to sleep (executed, I called it).

Cross-examination with the children became a necessity, and I would have learned that even if I had never been a lawyer. A case in point is Keith's early trip to see the scary movie, The Exorcist. He arrived home late. "Where were you, Keith?" "I was downtown." "What were you doing?" "Just kind of hanging around."

"Why didn't you call and tell us where you were?" "I had no money." "Keith, at this hour of the night, how did you get home?" "I took the bus." "Aha, a tissue of lies. If you had no money, how could you take the bus?" With that, Keith confessed to having found someone to buy him and his friend tickets to The Exorcist. He saw it, became frightened, and negotiated a ride home with a former prison guard. So traumatic was the movie—or maybe it was the cross-examination—that he slept in our room with a night-light on for about a week at his request.

Babysitters and downtown excursions seemed to be the category of harrowing adventures which come to light only bit by bit. When the children were very young, we were at the Colorado Bar Convention. The babysitter was priding herself on the great control she maintained over these four active children. Suddenly, the other three children watching television said, "There's Patrick!" "Don't be silly," replied the babysitter. But sure enough, there was Patrick on Channel 2. He had snuck out, somehow managed to get to the station and was appearing on a talkathon of some sort. Later, he explained that he thought he might win something. The babysitter could never explain what happened.

The most harrowing downtown excursions were done by the boys, not by Kyla. Their practice was to go to various downtown office buildings and to stop an elevator at a high floor. Somehow, they managed then to get on top of the elevator. They would spend the afternoon riding up and down the elevators, unbeknownst to anyone. They particularly liked the express elevators which skipped the first dozen or so floors, because the speed was much greater. Even today, Mary Ann and I have visions of their being squashed against the top of the elevator shaft, or wedged between fast-moving elevators. As it turned out, what we didn't know didn't hurt us—at the time.

As their high school years approached, all of the children broadened their horizons far beyond those which Mary Ann and I had experienced at their ages. Patrick engaged in construction and a series of jobs, traveled, and before starting law school, had visited more countries in Europe than I have seen. He once sent a letter from Budapest, announcing that he was on his way to Morocco, and that "I feel free!" I told Mary Ann that I would feel free too if I were in Budapest on my way to Morocco, without a care in the world.

Keith cut a wide swath through both Mexico and Europe. We never did get a full story of his college trip to Europe, except that it was clear he met virtually every girl on the continent, plus all those traveling from this hemisphere.

On Senior Seminar, an East High School program, Brian developed a deep appreciation for the environment. He also disobeyed some rule on the trip and managed to bring his grade average, as a result of that infraction, down to 3.98. His own college trip to Europe was particularly interesting because he traveled alone. As is the law of unintended consequences, he met and traveled with more different people than one could imagine.

As is often the case with the youngest, Kyla is the Marco Polo of the family. She has traveled on more than one occasion to Mexico. When she was barely sixteen, she spent the summer in the jungles of Honduras, living in villages where English was not spoken and where there was no electricity (at least in her first village) and little connection with the outside world. She spent the summer there building latrines in a public health program, often alone or at most with one other American student. In the evenings she organized and taught an English class to young Honduran children. During all that time, knowing the risk of infection and seeing children and animals dying, she never drank the water, notwithstanding the tremendous heat and thirst.

The following year, she went to Japan on a People-to-People exchange. With all these experiences, she has developed a great interest in the medical field. As a senior in high school, she spent a semester as an executive intern at St. Luke's Hospital. On at least one occasion I remember her saying, "I'm exhausted, I've been in surgery all day." And she had.

I never had a knack for fixing anything, under any circumstance. I did once remove a hook from the front door and put it on the back door, and that not very artfully.

Being handy with tools was something the children never learned, at least not from me. They probably thought that using a spoon to put on the license plates is the way it is supposed to be done. Part of that, however, is their own fault. On those rare occasions when tools were bought, they vanished. It's no wonder that no one knew the difference between a screwdriver and a pair of pliers.

There is not space in a chapter to do more than give these examples as a flavor of the daily activity in a busy household. All this was complicated by politics. Generally, the children were outstanding. However, on one occasion Patrick almost caused a civil war within the Democratic Party.

The year was 1966 and I was Chairman of the Denver Democratic Party. Patrick, then seven years old, wanted to go with me one Sunday to a meeting at Mike Pomponio's headquarters with a group of Italian-American Democrats in Northwest Denver.

After I had spoken and the applause had stopped, there is always a brief silence. At precisely that time, Patrick said loudly, "Dad, where are all the crooks?" There was no way to explain that comment to a group of aging Italian-Americans. I tried to explain that he must have been thinking about capital punishment, which I had discussed with him on the way over. That didn't help. He repeated the question. It took some time before the chill of my relationship with some of those good Italian-American Democrats had warmed. On the way home that day, I asked Patrick what in the world he was thinking. He explained that he was looking at all the pictures in the room, and said they looked like crooks. "Those were all former Democratic presidents!" I advised him sternly.

Whether I won or lost an election (and I did each about equally), the children were always with us, either at the victory celebration or for the concession speech. In the process, they learned the exhilaration of victory and the agony of defeat, that the world goes on, and that how the game is played is, in the long run, as important as the goal achieved.

We now have four in college at once—the product of our carefully planned parenthood. Fortunately, they are all at the University of Colorado, or this book would have a chapter on bankruptcy. There is no greater experience in the world than to grow up with magnificent and active children.

# III

# POLITICAL MATTERS, PARTISAN AND OTHERWISE

Dale, when Denver Democratic Chairman, with Bill Grant, Sen. Robert Kennedy and U.S. Attorney Lawrence Henry.

The 1971 Mayoralty campaign poster.

At the White House, 1980, with President Carter and Vice President Mondale.

Dale looks like the winner, but in fact he's conceding to Mayor Bill McNichols in 1975.

Campaigns aren't entirely speeches and handshakes.

# Chapter 6

# The Democratic Party

*Dale Tooley was not a typical politician, even though to many he appeared as one. He proved that one can disagree without being disagreeable. He brought out the best in both Democrats and Republicans.*

*His one dream, his one overpowering goal—of being Mayor of Denver—he never achieved. Yet, in seeking his life-long goal he led a fuller, more productive life in his 51 years than most of us could hope to accomplish in three lives.*

*It was always fun to be with Dale. I remember our trying to meet every Irish cop in the New York Police Department during the 1976 Democratic National Convention.*

— **Richard E. Young**

My association with the Democratic Party began when I persuaded Mary Ann, shortly after our marriage, to register as a Democrat. As we walked out of the clerk's office in Boulder, she said, "You know, it made me feel kind of sick," a statement from a girl born and raised in a Republican family in Sioux City, Iowa.

In 1962 I was nominated in a contested race to be a Democratic candidate for Regent of the University of Colorado. It was largely an alphabetical game, and 1962 was a tough year for Democrats. The Republicans swept the state, including the Regents contests. However, that race resulted in my being appointed a captain at large of the Denver Democratic Party. I ran for and in 1964 was elected party secretary.

In that position, we pioneered fund raising and pledge campaigns and did a great deal to bring the party's practices out of the 1800's. In 1966, I was elected Chairman of the Democratic Party in Denver, and was reelected in 1968.

Presiding over a diverse and large Democratic Party took more statesmanship than any public office. Notwithstanding that, we managed to eliminate the archaic practice of assessing candidates money for the right to spend their money to run for public office. We divided the districts in Denver to break the lock which district captains (bosses) traditionally had on the nominating process. In the process we were able to unify the party so that the vast majority of Democratic candidates in Denver won both years. In fact, the party had much to do with the reelection of Mayor Tom Currigan in 1967, since we were the entire field organization for that effort.

In September of 1968, we managed to persuade the Republicans not to oppose a proposal to amend the City Charter to call a spade a spade—that is, to have the two parties handle the municipal nominating process and the campaigns in the same way the Colorado party processes had functioned so well at the state level over the years. The amendment was overwhelmingly adopted by the voters, but was subsequently thrown out in a political decision by the Colorado Supreme Court, based upon an allegedly confusing ballot title drawn by the city attorney's office, which never had liked the idea.

The year of 1968 had to be the most traumatic year in the history of American politics. That was the year in which Martin Luther King, Jr. and Robert Kennedy were both assassinated. It was the year that rioters put the torch to Washington, D.C. It was still a high point in the civil rights movement, and the national protest against the war in Viet Nam had turned brother against brother, split families and caused young men to go into hiding in Canada and to evade the draft under penalty of imprisonment.

I organized the First Congressional District (Denver) Convention, which as party chairman was my responsibility. I made it clear that it was what Presidential candidate one was for, not who a delegate candidate was, which mattered. It was a very democratic process. A coalition of Eugene McCarthy and Robert Kennedy backers swept the convention, while the Hubert Humphrey supporters, although constituting a plurality, were elected as alternates. As an alternate, I went to the 1968 convention in Chicago.

Politics in Denver and in Colorado is very clean compared

to Chicago and many areas in the East. To view the practices of Mayor Daley was an eye-opener. When he announced that he would brook no disturbances, it was an overt signal to the Chicago police to attack protesters in Grant Park in downtown Chicago. On our way to the convention hall each day, our buses were required to drive through his precinct, where the fronts but not the sides of the houses had been freshly painted, and where children stood outside, lining the streets, with American flags and signs saying "We love you Mayor Daley." It was heavy. The convention itself was like an armed camp, but the party survived, and Hubert Humphrey came remarkably close to defeating Richard Nixon in November. That experience, as much as any in my political life, convinced me of the need for reform.

The demonstrators were not without some excesses, as well. I watched a group of young demonstrators lounging under a tree. As soon as a network television crew arrived, they jumped to their feet and began engaging in a melee. On another occasion, I recall returning to our hotel after a long session at the convention hall, to find newspapers already published by one of the anti-war groups, dated the next day and reporting on the riots which had "occurred" the next day. Nevertheless, but for those young people and those demonstrators we might not have extricated this country from the folly of the Viet Nam War.

The convention sessions sometimes ran until three in the morning. I listened intently to Sorenson and the other speakers debate the Viet Nam War issue. I was convinced, based upon the facts presented, that Vice President Humphrey was more correct about the war than were the demonstrators. Even at that, some of us from the Colorado delegation urged him to select a running mate who would be more acceptable to the anti-war faction, such as the Republican Mayor of New York, John Lindsay. It was a glove-tight election, and had he done so, he might well have been President and the Nixon Watergate era would never have darkened our country's history.

Later, the Pentagon Papers came out, and it became apparent to me for the first time that those young demonstrators in Chicago and across the land were right, and that we were wrong on the Viet Nam War. I became angry that the restriction of news had led me and millions of other Americans to an incorrect conclusion, particularly at a time when I was having some degree of contact with those who were in top decision-making positions of the government. I did not make that mistake again. Eleven years later, while talking with President Carter at the White House, I made a point of underscoring my support for his goal of bringing the hostages in Iran home without starting World War III. It's too bad it took me so long to learn.

In 1969 and 1970, I headed the Reform Commission of the Colorado Democratic Party, in which we participated in the reform of the delegate selection process. Actually, it was in that context that I introduced Gary Hart, then a young Denver lawyer, to Senator George McGovern, who would in 1972 be the Democratic nominee for President.

I ran into Gary Hart on Seventeenth Street one day and invited him to the Reform Commission hearings at the Hilton Hotel. He said he was busy but that he might come by, and I invited him to come for lunch to meet this "guy named McGovern, from South Dakota." He came to the luncheon and met McGovern. Later, McGovern asked what I knew about Gary Hart. "Very bright young lawyer. He's a very good man," I replied. He then asked Gary to advance some Reform Commission hearings elsewhere.

Not long after that Gary called and asked to go to lunch. He said that McGovern had asked him to be involved in McGovern's campaign for the Democratic Presidential nomination. My track record in predicting victories is not all that great. I remember vividly saying to Gary, "Take my word for it. He will never be our nominee for President. However, if it's something you want to do, just make sure that you're running the show." Either he took that advice, or would have done it anyway, but he headed the McGovern campaign and was the mastermind behind the McGovern sweep of the 1972 Convention. That position made Hart a legitimate candidate in the U.S. Senate race in Colorado in 1974, which he won and after which he himself would almost become the Democratic Presidential nominee in 1984.

My apprehensions about Senator McGovern, as well meaning as he was, arose in part out of a meeting at the Albany Hotel in Denver in 1970. Hart had gathered 20 or 30 Democratic Party leaders together to meet with McGovern. After a long discussion I said, "Senator, issues come and issues go. Let me ask you this: if you are elected President, how will you govern the country? How will you relate to the Congress and the American people? In short, how will you conduct the office of President?"

McGovern paused for what was probably only 30 seconds, but for what seemed like five minutes. He slowly replied, "Well, I might let more people into the White House to talk to me. Frankly, that's a question I have never really thought about." In my view, that should have been the first question a candidate should have thought about—namely, how to conduct the office he seeks.

In the summer of 1968, Tom Currigan made known to me that he planned to resign as Mayor, in part because the Mayor was then earning only $14,000 per year, and in part because he had an offer to go to work as a Vice President of Continental Airlines. In August, he asked that I succeed him, which he could do since succession to the office was essentially by a Mayor's appointment. Whoever the Mayor appointed as Manager of Public Works was Depty Mayor and successor in the event of a resignation or a vacancy. I initially said I was not interested, but ultimately said I would do it. As a consequence, I resigned as chairman of the party immediately following the November, 1968, elections, declining to do so earlier because I felt that completing the election was part of the responsibility I had undertaken when I was reelected as chairman.

Only a week before the resignation of Currigan was to be announced, Mary Ann and I had dinner with a Currigan supporter, one of the few who knew of the forthcoming resignation. During that conversation, in an exchange which I considered insignificant at the time, there was a discussion about Denver's airport. I allowed that I did not like what I considered a certain number of "sweetheart contracts" with the airlines, that I thought the landing fees ought to be adjusted, and that the airport should be as much a function of city government as any other part of the government of the City and County of Denver. I also said that while as Mayor I would be willing to restore Bill McNichols as Manager of Public Works (under whose jurisdiction the airport fell), I would not agree to tenure for him.

Within a day or two after that conversation, Tom Currigan began having apprehensions about his changing the succession from then Manager of Public Works—Bill McNichols—to me.

I thought his apprehensions had some good basis, and I ultimately suggested that if it were to go forward, it should be done with a special election, to make it clear that the public participated in the process. That could easily have been done by my consent as the successor.

There followed any number of conversations between Currigan and Continental Airlines officials. It finally became apparent to both of us that "this dog won't hunt." Currigan and Continental Airlines did not like the idea of a special election. That is my story of the Currigan resignation—except for what I still don't know about the effect of my candid comments about how the airport ought to be run.

Attending a national political convention is something everyone should do once or twice in a lifetime—but not more. In 1980, I was the first Colorado delegate elected, pledged to support President Carter. A key issue in the convention was whether it would be an open convention, where delegates could vote their consciences, or whether delegates were bound by the candidate for whom they had announced their support. The Carter organization was adamant that this was a pro- or anti-Carter vote, and that it was the only way to prevent the nomination from going to Senator Edward Kennedy. My view was just the opposite. I knew many delegates. They had to go home after the convention. Few, if any, would ever change their allegiances, and I felt the public would better accept the nomination if it were done in an open convention rather than in one the press was describing as closed.

Mary Anne Castellano, an assistant of mine at the Denver District Attorney's Office, and I were the two Colorado Carter delegates who voted for an open convention. A direct result of that vote was that my seat was moved from the aisle to the center of the delegation. Politics is not bean bag.

Also, as ethical and decent an administration as Jimmy Carter ran, there was pressure to vote with his organization on this issue. One high budget official of the Carter administration called on me in the delegation. He knew that I was then serving as Denver district attorney, and that through hard work we had obtained more than $2 million of Law Enforcement Assistance Administration grants from the Justice Department—more than any other prosecutor's office in the Rocky Mountain West. He pointedly reminded me of this, and the fact that those funds were not guaranteed. He then got into the discussion of how important it was that I vote against the open convention resolution. I explained that I didn't need federal money to conduct my office, anyway. In fact, I had accepted the last grant I intended to seek because the red tape was so tremendous and the needs of the office were by then well funded. Nevertheless, that less-than-veiled threat is a reminder that there is always a tendency for power to corrupt, and as the saying goes, for absolute power to corrupt absolutely.

No one ever described the Democratic Party better than Will Rogers, who declared, "I am not a member of an organized political party. I am a Democrat."

## Chapter 7

# Campaigns For Mayor

*Dale had a quietly ebullient personality combined with enormous energy and the toughest of hides.*

*He enjoyed people, met them easily, and was always interested in what they had to say even when the conversation took place in the midst of a hectic campaign schedule. During his many campaigns he constantly incorporated what he learned from these brief encounters into his thinking and actions.*

*He never backed away from the political hard ones. Those tough walks to give concession speeches, and facing 200 angry police officers in front of his campaign headquarters in a controversy over hollow point bullets come to mind. The same was true of personal hard ones, particularly making the most positive of statements out of his own terminal illness. He really participated in his life.*

— **Hugh J. McClearn**

We began the 1971 campaign for mayor with a name identification level of only 2 percent, according to our polls. The odds were astronomical. The incumbent mayor, Bill McNichols, who succeeded Currigan when he resigned, was the brother of the former Governor of Colorado, Steve McNichols. Ironically, McNichols became Mayor out of an arrangement originally orchestrated through the late North Denver Democratic District Captain, Mike Pomponio. Pomponio got the word to Currigan during Currigan's initial 1963 campaign that unless Currigan made Bill McNichols Manager of Public Works, Steve McNichols might consider running for mayor. The ploy worked, and Bill McNichols served as Manager of Public Works and Deputy Mayor during all of Currigan's tenure.

The first campaign was an uphill battle all the way. I began to walk the city, from Adams County on the north to Arapahoe County on the south, across the city from west to east, and back again. In the process, we handed out "Tooley trees," which were small saplings designed to help beautify the city—and to help voters remember who I was. Even today, citizens come up to me commenting on the height of their Tooley tree.

The walk across the city was a good experience. About the first block, I said to a filling station operator, "My name is Dale Tooley and I'm running for Mayor." His immediate response was: "You must not be too bright if you want that job."

On another occasion, I walked into a beauty parlor, which I was never to do again while campaigning. All the women had their hair in various contortions, and were clearly uncomfortable with a man prowling their territory. I noticed that one woman was removing the hair dryer hood and another woman who had been waiting stood up, I assumed to take her place. I said to the woman waiting: "Well, it looks like it's your turn." She shot back icily: "I've already been."

My good friend Richard Young skillfully managed the campaign, and Velma Andrews, who was to become my administrative assistant as district attorney, was a master at running the campaign headquarters. It was a massive volunteer effort. We raised $100,000, spent $123,000, and incurred a deficit I personally assumed and paid off. Deficits in fact belong, and should belong, to the candidate.

McNichols was far better financed.

On the first election night, to the surprise of the pundits, and pollsters, I led the field. The third mayoral candidate, Replublican State Senator Joe Shoemaker, ran last, but he ran a classy and ethical campaign. The first-round win gave us tremendous momentum, particularly since the McNichols forces had banked on running first, having knocked out in court the partisan election charter amendment which the voters had unanimously approved, and which would have clearly relegated McNichols to an also-ran. He had little support within the Democratic Party structure, and I had just been the party's chairman for two terms.

On the Sunday before the runoff election, the *Denver Post* poll had me leading McNichols by a margin of three to two, which is landslide proportions. This was later repeated in the absentee ballot count (absentee ballots could be cast only through Friday before the Tuesday election), which I carried by an overwhelming margin. However, the McNichols public relations people seized upon a brilliant, effective and probably the most disreputable campaign tactic in modern Denver political history.

Busing had been an important and volatile issue in the Denver school system. I had no particular involvement in the lawsuit which brought about the mandatory busing for integration, and it was not an issue in the mayor's race because the school board is separately elected and the mayor has no power over the Board of Education.

The lawyer who helped lead the busing efforts in the courts was Craig Barnes, later to be a candidate for Congress. Barnes was a supporter and friend of mine, but not an active participant in the campaign.

Just before the runoff election, full-page ads appeared urging defeat of the "Tooley-Barnes Bunch." The same theme was carried out by telephone bank calls, particularly to Republican and unaffiliated voters. The net result was a victory by McNichols of less than 2,000 votes in one of the closest mayoral elections in history.

On election night, as I always felt was protocol and a showing of respect for the system, Mary Ann, the children and I went to McNichols headquarters in the Hilton Hotel. We were treated boorishly by the crowd as I gave a concession speech which was conciliatory. That night helped the children know how to be a good loser—and how to be a poor winner.

Because of the closeness of the 1971 campaign, and because I had been overwhelmingly elected district attorney, defeating the Republican incumbent in 1972, it was inevitable that I would be a candidate a second time against McNichols in 1975.

This campaign was conducted out of a large headquarters at Eleventh Avenue and Broadway in a former automobile dealership. Ironically, the dealership had been that of Russ Vento, a crooked car dealer whom we had convicted and I had run out of business—although he was not the building landlord. Again, thousands of volunteers were involved, but I conducted both the District Attorney's Office and the campaign at the same time. That, I learned, was a mistake. It was almost impossible to insulate all of the decisions as district attorney from appearing to be political positions, and the time pressures were extraordinary. Nevertheless, we went to the shopping centers, attended rallies, made speeches and did all those things which we had done in 1971.

Peter McLaughlin, an innovative realtor and former Regis College professor, managed the campaign well, and my friend Pat Shannon Havekost served well as campaign chairperson.

One day while at a shopping center on Federal Boulevard in West Denver, an older lady walked out with an attractive young person. I said to her, "What an attractive granddaughter." She replied brusquely, "That is my son." "Well, he looks bright," I said. "He's retarded," she retorted. I doubt that I got her vote, and I never made such assumptions again.

Remembering names is important in a political campaign, and I became rather proficient at it. I often used word associations as a tool, until at a Capitol Hill rally one evening I entered and met a man named Mr. Woodchuck. As I left the reception, he was still standing by the door and I said to him, "I'm glad to have met you, Mr. Chipmunk."

Having grown up in Denver, it is not uncommon to run into people who knew me when I was a child. One lady at a South Denver shopping area came up to me and pleasantly said, "I'm not going to vote for you." "Why?" I asked. "Because," she replied, "I lived up the street from you on Downing, and one time when you were a little boy, you threw a baseball, broke a window in my house and blamed it on your little brother."

I disclaimed memory of the incident, which I still don't recall. That didn't suffice. I said maybe my older brother did it and blamed me. That didn't work, either. Finally, in desperation, I said, "Doesn't the statute of limitations ever run out on such events?" "Not at all," she said. "People never change."

The irony of the 1975 campaign was that, just before the campaign began, a Denver police officer, using hollow point bullets, had shot and badly wounded an innocent citizen. Hollow point bullets have a particular impact and destructive capacity when they strike the human flesh. As district attorney, I announced that I thought use of hollow point bullets should be suspended until they were studied further to see if they were really necessary for the protection of the police officers. This was a very sore point with the police. Just a few days before my campaign kickoff, a Denver police officer was shot and killed—with a hollow point bullet (although he was struck in the heart, and any kind of bullet would have killed him). The officer's funeral was the same day as the campaign kickoff, and several hundred officers appeared, in an emotional state, at my campaign headquarters, protesting what they had understood to be my opposition to all use of hollow point bullets by officers. That fringe issue seemed to have a life of its own during the course of the campaign.

I won the first election, running ahead of McNichols, and eliminating Charles Byrne, the capable Republican auditor who was the third major candidate for mayor. Before the runoff election, Byrne endorsed my candidacy, but McNichols won the election and I again found myself making the long walk to the McNichols headquarters and conceding defeat as graciously as I knew how. This time, the crowd was not boorish and McNichols' conduct was appropriate.

In the 1975 campaign, a city ordinance had been adopted, placing a maximum campaign expenditure limit of $120,000. We easily raised that amount, and had several thousand dollars left over, which we donated to Joe Shoemaker's Platte River beautification project. In 1971, a legacy was trees, and in 1975 a legacy was Platte River beautification.

My final campaign in the quest for Mayor was 1983. I had been reelected district attorney in 1976 without opposition, which had never before happened in the history of the city. In 1980, I was reelected to a third term as district attorney, carrying 64 percent of the vote and leading the Democratic ticket in Denver. However, I had learned from the 1975 campaign that it was impossible to do justice to both the conduct of the District Attorney's Office and the mayorality campaign at the same time. Therefore, in November, 1982, I announced to my staff and to the public that I would be resigning as district attorney within 90 days in order to devote my full efforts to my candidacy for mayor.

This was a massive campaign. More than 4,000 volunteers were involved. Computers were used. We raised and expended three-quarters of a million dollars in the campaign. Hugh McClearn, with whom I had practiced law, was an excellent campaign manager, and Pat Knous was the skillful campaign coordinator. My son Keith took six months off and did a superb job as assistant to Pat Knous. I got to know him and the other children better as a result of each campaign.

The campaign involved all of the elements that the previous campaign had included, and more so. I gave 356 speeches, including 118 events which were debates or joint appearances with the other four major candidates.

The candidates included Mayor McNichols, who ran a low-key campaign. Federico Peña, former minority leader in the Colorado House of Representatives, ran an aggressive campaign which was not terribly specific, but which had the image of being quite detailed. Wellington Webb, a leader in the Black community, former legislator and former member of Governor Richard Lamm's cabinet, was in the race with vigor, as was Monte Pascoe, former Democratic Party state chairman and also a former member of Lamm's cabinet. Other candidates were Steve Schweitzberger, a maverick, and Harold Sudmeyer, a Socialist Workers Party candidate. It was a circus.

The May election brought surprising results. Peña, the newcomer, ran first, probably because McNichols and I split much of the same vote, and because the other candidates were of almost no effect, each garnering less than 10% of the vote. I ran second, so the runoff election was between me and Peña. Finally, I had defeated Bill McNichols by a substantial margin, including having rolled up large margins of victory over him in his previous strongholds. Neither he nor the other defeated candidates made the expected trip to congratulate the winners, a traditional showing of respect for our elective system.

The last month of the campaign was as hectic as any campaign. It proved to be the largest and most expensive campaign in the history of the city. To keep the campaign on a high plane, we used the theme, "Two good men are running for Mayor, but there are substantial differences between us." We enumerated those differences and those issues.

Peña enjoyed an overwhelming lead in the polls following his strong finish in the first election. The polls indicated that we were coming up fast. However, the day after the initial election, by a fluke of the calendar which had never before occurred, there were several days of new voter registrations permitted. Peña's organization registered some 6,000 new voters, almost all of them Hispanics. There remained a strong suspicion and some evidence that many of them were not citizens, but that could never clearly be established, and I declined to make it an issue. Those new registrations proved to be more than enough to make a difference.

It was a campaign with shifting alliances from previous campaigns. In June, a number of leading Republicans took me and Pat Knous to lunch. They asked for permission to use our telephone bank, "to do to Peña what they had done to me in 1971." I asked what they had in mind. They said they wanted to call every registered Republican, and as many unaffiliated voters as they could, to give the message that if Peña were elected, Denver would become an "open city," overrun by Mexican nationals. They said I would not have to know about the message and would have nothing to do with it.

My response was immediate. "It's not going to happen. I don't believe it, and despite the fact that it would probably make the difference in the campaign, it is not the right way to conduct a campaign." I told them "no" in no uncertain terms. That message and those tactics were never used.

The Saturday before the Tuesday runoff election, I was on a platform at a celebration in the Five Points area, a predominately Black section of Denver. Chris Munch, one of my chief deputies, came to the podium and told me my mother had suffered another heart attack and was critical. I immediately left and found my mother in a near-death situation at her home. I promptly called for an ambulance and took charge enough to persuade her to go to the hospital while there was still a chance. As she was being rolled to the ambulance, she almost expired. To this day, I can remember seeing that event and looking at the anguished expressions on the faces of my children as they watched the near-tragedy unfolding.

As mother has always said, we are a family of fighters. She was taken to the hospital and recovered. I felt it appropriate to suspend all further campaigning, as did Peña, and our final two television debates were scratched. However, the sympathy and tragedy of that situation did not affect the campaign.

Election night rolled around with swift results. They always come in more quickly than one would expect after so long a campaign. With one-fourth of the vote counted, I was ahead.

I finally carried a majority of the precincts in Denver, but lost by 4,000 votes. I garnered more than 75,000 votes, which no one had ever done before without being elected. Peña had carried the Black and Hispanic precincts by such large margins that even though he lost most of the city's precincts, he won the race. His registration of those additional six thousand voters more than made the difference.

I promptly went to Currigan Hall to congratulate him and did so with as much grace as I could muster. By then I had become pretty good at giving concession speeches. Again, my children were there with me. We had succeeded in conducting a massive campaign without once bringing in race as an issue, and without using any of the tactics of the kind the McNichols campaign had successfully used in 1971 in a similar situation. I would rather have lost without such tactics than won by using them.

That campaign ended my quest for mayor, although so many of the issues and programs I advocated in those three campaigns came to pass—from administrative reforms to campaign funds disclosure to adoption of a system for retention of judges and many, many more.

In no other ventures could one meet and come to know such a broad cross section of our society. They were all battles worth fighting, and I had no regrets, except that having both won and lost major races, I know that winning is far more comfortable than losing.

The campaigns also served to illustrate the old adage that it is impossible to see into the future. The 1971 campaign would have turned out differently but for the "Tooley-Barnes Bunch" last-minute tactics and but for the sloppiness of the City Attorney's office in writing the ballot title to the partisan election charter amendment. The 1975 campaign might have turned out differently had a young thug not killed a police officer with a hollow point bullet. The 1983 campaign would certainly have had a different result had there not been a special week of additional registration permitting the Peña organization to add 6,000 additional people to the voting lists at the last minute. But who would want a system where one could see into the future?

# IV

# TRAVELS ABROAD

Dale arriving in Tashkent, U.S.S.R., in 1978.

In Bethlehem, in 1979, Dale finds the Israeli soldiers friendly.

The Tooleys and the Wongs, in Wuxi, Peoples' Republic of China, 1981.

# Chapter 8

# Other Systems of Justice

As tourists, Mary Ann and I, and sometimes the children, have visited Mexico City, the west coast of Mexico, Cozumel, the Yucatan, Hawaii, Alaska, France, Greece, England and Italy. Still, the most fascinating trips were those connected with a delegation, and serving in public office provided some unique opportunities.

In 1974, we traveled on a National District Attorneys Association charter to Ireland. The Attorney General of Ireland took us to observe a routine trial of a young man named Timothy O'Connor. O'Connor was charged with violation of the Crimes Against the State Act, which meant he was alleged to be a member of the Irish Republican Army (IRA).

The case was tried in an old courtroom in Dublin, adjacent to the prison. Before the trial, we met with the three-judge panel which would hear the case. The presiding judge said, "Well, if O'Connor fights it, it may take forty-five minutes. Otherwise, it will be over in short order." I assumed this meant it was a preliminary hearing to determine if there would be probable cause to hold O'Connor for trial.

O'Connor was brought into the courtroom in chains, and he faced the court without counsel, which was his choice. "How do you plead, Mr. O'Connor?" asked the presiding judge. "Not guilty, Your Honor," replied O'Connor. With that, the proceedings began.

The Crown called three witnesses, each of whom testified simply that O'Connor was "believed" to be a member of the IRA. When O'Connor asked each witness, "On what do you base that belief?", there was an immediate objection by the counsel for the crown. "Objection! We claim the privilege."

"Sustained, let's get on with it, Mr. O'Connor," barked the judge.

O'Connor asked one of the police witnesses, "As I have a

twin brother, how do you know it is not my brother rather than I who is supposed to be a member of the IRA?"

"Objection!"

"Sustained. We're wasting time Mr. O'Connor," responded the judge. As predicted, the proceedings took about forty-five minutes and with no more testimony than I have described, the panel left to deliberate.

They returned to the courtroom, brought O'Connor to attention, and sentenced him to one year in prison, which he summarily began serving as they removed him from the courtroom. I was outraged.

I spoke to a young man in the courtroom whom I assumed was an Irish attorney. "This is outrageous. Why, in the United States, that amount of evidence would not be enough even to meet the requirements of a preliminary hearing," I charged. The young man pulled out a pad and pencil and began taking notes and asking questions. I soon realized I was talking to a member of the Irish Free Press. The next day, there was a story headlined: "American Prosecutor Blasts Irish System of Justice."

I asked the Attorney General of Ireland if there was a presumption of innocence in Ireland. "Oh, yes," he replied, "in almost all cases, but not in special cases like this." He then had us observe a burglary trial where there were all of the safeguards which we take for granted. However, the test of a judicial system is how it handles the "special" cases—the high, hard ones—not how it handles garden variety burglary trials. In my mind, Ireland's system of justice had failed that test, notwithstanding their understandable fear of terrorism. It was, however, refreshing to observe a murder trial in Old Bailey Courthouse in London a week later, where all the precautions we take for granted were present, and where the presumption of innocence was alive and well.

In 1978 I was invited to be a member of a delegation of a dozen district attorneys to visit the Soviet Union. We were to be guests of the Soviet government, with an exchange visit later by our Russian counterparts. We told the Soviet authorities that we wanted to meet with Soviet officials at the highest level to discuss with them the plight of Soviet Jews who were discriminated against, persecuted and arbitrarily denied exit visas, in clear violation of the Final Chapter of the Helsinki Accords. They must not have realized what we were saying, because they approved the delegation, anyway.

In the Soviet Union we actually did meet with Soviet officials at the highest level—often in heated exchanges. We had a particularly confrontational meeting with Roman Rudenko, then Procurator General of the Soviet Union. Rudenko was a tough old Communist who had been the chief Soviet prosecutor at the Nuremberg war crimes trials after World War II. We had prepared well, and interrogated him in detail about the Anatoly Scharansky and other cases. He explained that these were "special cases" and that they were treated differently than regular cases.

We found that to be true, that there were two faces of justice in the Soviet Union—one for average cases and the other for special cases. Special cases were those involving confrontations with the power of the government, those involving Soviet Jews seeking to emigrate, and those in which the Western press had taken an interest.

Our efforts apparently had more impact than we realized. Then-President Leonid Brezhnev gave a speech in the Central Asian part of the Soviet Union, answering many of the charges which we had made in our meetings in Moscow. The following year, the number of exit visas granted to Soviet Jews was the highest in the history of the Soviet Union. We believe we had some impact on that result.

Under the Soviet system, procurators supervise the legality of the entire government, and are much like godfathers. The Soviets assumed we had comparable power, and we never had occasion to tell them to the contrary. As a result, we were treated with limousine caravans, special flights and all the "perks" of visiting dignitaries. With that status, we were free to meet evenings in the various cities with groups of refuseniks—generally Soviet Jews who had been denied exit visas, fired from their jobs for seeking them and then often harassed or prosecuted for being without employment (parasites). Some of those with whom we met were subsequently allowed to leave Russia. Because of our freedom and status, we were able to bring to the refuseniks letters, bibles, and other publications which were otherwise prohibited in the Soviet Union.

Even that part of the Soviet system which dealt with regular cases was not objective by our standards. I asked one Soviet procurator, "How long does it take for a criminal case to move through your system?" His reply was, "Our cases move in 90 days from arrest to *conviction*." I then began inquiring if any procurator had ever known of an acquittal, and none could recall one.

The Soviets often simply define away their problems. I asked a Deputy Procurator General about the proliferation of prostitutes around Red Square. He denied that there were any prostitutes in the Soviet Union. I reminded him that we had observed many of them on the street the night before. His reply was, "Oh, those. Those are not prostitutes. Those are parasites who have no useful employment. We have no prostitution problem in the Soviet Union."

The Soviets did, however, admit to a massive alcoholism problem. The depth of the problem is illustrated by our visit to an Institute for Crime Prevention, where we discussed alcoholism. The morning session on alcoholism was interrupted so that we could be served vodka and have toasts all around as we were discussing the acute alcoholism problem.

In Odessa, I met at an opera a young Russian couple, Alexis and Nina. They were computer operators for the Soviet maritime agency. They were treated rudely by our Soviet hosts because they were talking to Westerners. I arranged to meet them in a park following the opera and the evening banquet. They said, "Are you the American delegation?" "What American delegation?" I inquired. "The American delegation which came in from the airport two nights ago." I replied that we were, and they thanked me profusely. They said that they had attempted to have their apartments painted for a number of years, and it was not until our delegation was coming that the Soviets painted the apartments along the route we traveled from the airport to our hotel in central Odessa.

It is an insecure country.

Its insecurity is perhaps best demonstrated by this scenerio which occurred on an airplane en route to Uzbekistan, a Central Asian republic of the Soviet Union. I was reading the English translation of the new Soviet Constitution. It said that the Socialist principle is "from each according to his ability, to each according to his *work*." I asked one of the high Soviet officials if that was a misprint, because Marx had written, "from each according to his ability, to each according to his *need*." The official was without an answer, and huddled with other officials in the back of the aircraft. Half an hour later he came forward to say, "It is not a misprint. We hope someday to achieve what Marx is saying, but how do you get people to work if you do not provide an incentive?" He could scarcely defend against my accusation that he was a closet capitalist.

As is so often the case, the government may be standing in the way of the people in the sense that the Soviet people do not seem warlike, but the government seems unresponsive and paranoid. If there is to be peace between our countries, it will be aided by greater exchanges between the peoples of both nations. We never lose in those exchanges.

The trip which was the most fascinating to Mary Ann and equally fascinating to me was our trip with a delegation of district attorneys to Israel. Even in Israel, however, with its dedication to human rights and its laudable democratic traditions, special cases sometimes cause suspension of usual protections of civil liberties. Some 30 persons prior to our visit in 1979 were held, without charges and without trial, under administrative detention. However, with that exception, the Israeli system of justice seemed exemplary. Justice Ahron Barak of the Israeli Supreme Court, the former Attorney General of Israel, met with us at length to discuss the system and to explain why their traditions provide no jury trial, but otherwise include the protections built into the British system of justice. The irony is that the procedures may be British, but the law applied is often Turkish, Arabic or Jewish, depending upon the nature of the matter and the area of Israel involved.

While in Israel, we visited the massive Arab refugee camps in the Gaza Strip. It seemed like the kind of problem that ought to be solvable, except that there is so little land and so many competing for it. However, our luncheon was hosted by a General of the Israeli army who explained that his family had lived in Gaza for 400 years, and that the Israeli view of roots and tradition was far different than we could comprehend.

It became apparent that within a few miles there would be a Jewish town and an Arab town, and yet the Israeli government permits all citizens to vote equally, whether Arab or Jew.

The Israeli government also makes heroic efforts to absorb

Jewish refugees from other countries.

While in Jerusalem, we met Wolf Zalmanson, one of the recently-released refuseniks who had been prosecuted and convicted in the famous Leningrad trials. Zalmanson's case was one of those which we had pressed in our meetings the year before in the Soviet Union, and who was released some months later along with six other refuseniks. The absorption centers taught language and skills, and generally brought the refugees into the Israeli mainstream far better than our country handled our own refugees through Ellis Island.

Visiting the bastion of Masada, where Jews perished rather than surrender to the Romans, visiting and swimming in the Dead Sea, and standing where tradition holds that Jesus gave his Sermon on the Mount near the Sea of Galilee were sights available to all travelers. What was not available and what we experienced was the vividness of the Arab-Jewish conflict in the north of Israel. We visited the Golan Heights, site of fierce battles between Israel and Syria, and the border of Lebanon. It was patroled by United Nations troops. They were a mixed lot. The Irish troops preferred to sunbathe in the nude, to the great consternation of the Jewish women. The Fiji troops literally arrived in grass skirts in a climate which does not welcome such dress. The best troops were Nepalese, but because they did their job so well their fatality rates were the highest.

Near Metulla we stayed in a kibbutz which had recently been attacked by Lebanese missiles. That night, Israeli tanks moved north from Metulla near our kibbutz, and the following day we observed Israeli jets making air strikes on Lebanese bases in southern Lebanon. The fact that the Israeli nation can continue to survive with such conflict with its neighbors is a tribute to the tenacity of the Israeli people. They deserve to survive and they deserve our support. More than that, they deserve our best efforts to preserve their existence, even if it means the loss of West Bank settlements or other necessary territorial compromises.

The only disappointment in all of Israel was that we could never find a bagel!

In many ways the most unique of any of our travels abroad was our trip to China. One afternoon in 1981 I received a call from Robert Johnson, former President of the National District Attorneys' Association. He said that he and his wife could not lead a delegation of district attorneys, judges and criminal justice experts to the People's Republic of China, as planned, and wondered if Mary Ann and I would do so. It took about ten seconds to say yes, indeed.

In October of that year we left first for Hong Kong, where we were the guests of Assistant Crown Prosecutor Thomas Gall. It was an opportunity to observe cases being tried, the system of justice in action and to see how the British in a colonial way had simply transposed their system of justice on this thriving Asiatic colony. It was in sharp contrast to the rules governing the teeming millions we saw when we left Hong Kong for Guangzhou (formerly Canton). It was in Guangzhou that our conflicts with the totalitarian Chinese government began. For some reason the Chinese were reluctant to allow us to inspect their system of justice, despite previous assurances that we would be able to do so. As leader of the delegation, I pressed the issue at every point, but it was like talking to a brick wall.

Our success was no better as we traveled north to Changsha, capital of Hunan Province. I decided to wait until we were at the seat of power in Beijing (formerly Peking) before more directly pressing the issue of accessibility to their system. It didn't take long. In short order we required our driver to take us to the Beijing courthouse. There, we staged a semi-demonstration, unheard of in China. Following a confrontation with Messrs. Gao and Yu at government offices in Beijing, a powerful woman named Mrs. Liu arrived late in the evening at our compound. At last, we had gotten their attention! She assigned to us a special guide, a remarkable woman by the name of Mrs. Wong, and the system suddenly became more accessible.

In Wuxi, we met with members of mediation committees. In China, there are 5.7 million mediators. They handle the vast majority of conflicts which in our system are handled in the courts. At one Wuxi commune with 18,000 people, of the 153 disputes the previous year all but two were resolved by mediation. The two that went to the courts were considered exceptions and failures of the mediation system. It became apparent that one reason for their reluctance to show us their legal system was that there is not much of a legal system in China.

During the cultural revolution the Chinese courts and system of justice were essentially shut down. This continued for almost

20 years. During the cultural revolution students and intellectuals were routinely persecuted and sent to the countryside to live in terror. The Chinese talk candidly about the errors of those times, and about the misguided leadership of the Gang of Four which caused the cultural revolution. At the time of our visit, the law schools were only beginning to reopen.

In Nanjing (previously Nanking) we met with Chinese law professors and with judges of the Chinese courts. By the time we reached Shanghai we had figured out the system well enough even to cause a change in the schedule and to have an extra passenger car added to a train in order to change our itinerary. In Shanghai we viewed what may have been a typical Chinese trial. It was more of a sentencing hearing than a trial.

The defendant had stolen 48 kilograms of welding rods and a batch of overalls from the factory where he worked. As he climbed out of the factory and was getting on his getaway bike he was apprehended. He blamed it mostly on his mother-in-law. He pleaded for mercy and was not incarcerated. Instead, he was, in effect, placed upon probation to the people. Instead of having one probation officer, he was placed under the supervision of the entire society. That would seem like a meaningless punishment in our culture, but in China, peer pressure is so great that the penalty was considered severe. Peer pressure is the glue which holds together the Chinese society.

Additional demands and diplomacy resulted in our being able to visit a prison in Shanghai, undoubtedly their best, but by our standards it would be our worst. According to the warden, the prisoners are required to work hard (from dawn until dark) so that the prison operates at a net operating profit. We could learn by that. At our request, we were able to see Chinese prisoners making clothes and other consumer goods. There were no laggards, and according to the Chinese authorities, few recidivists.

Although the Chinese officials talked in humanitarian terms, we learned of many cases where there were summary executions of criminals for serious crimes. The system might be effective, but it is brutal in a way that Chinese punishment has historically been brutal.

In our visits with Chinese citizens we did our best to convey the importance of freedom, of individual opportunity and of the desire for peace. Perhaps we planted a seed. We certainly did with our special guide, Mrs. Wong, who became fascinated with the adage "nothing ventured, nothing gained." For her boldness on our behalf she was disciplined, and I hope we did not create more far-reaching problems for her after we left. Nevertheless, even with the deprivation of rights, liberties and opportunities, the Chinese are at least well-fed and without the street crime which existed during Chiang's regime. To have had the opportunity to visit a country with a billion people was an experience of a lifetime. It also convinced me that I'd rather live in Denver.

# V

# A DECADE AS DISTRICT ATTORNEY

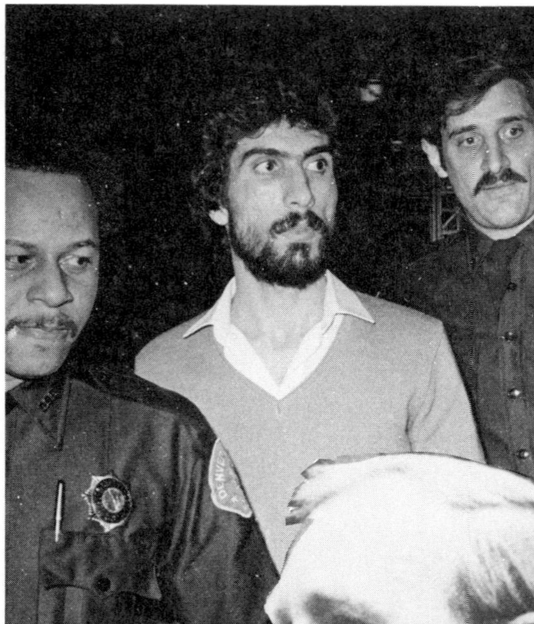

Above left, DA staffer Rand Hendrickson leads Bill Riley out of airliner in 1982. Above right, Afshin Shariati is ushered into court by a deputy in 1979. In photo on right, Dale makes a point in court.

Dale confers with his successor as district attorney, Norm Early in late 1982.

Former Colorado Supreme Court Chief Justice O. Otto Moore donned his robes to swear in Norm Early. Dale was an interested observer.

# Chapter 9

# Office of the District Attorney, 1973-1983

*When Dale first was elected and asked me to be his assistant at the Denver District Attorney's Office, I said that I didn't know anything about the D.A.'s Office or what made it run. He replied, "That's O.K. I've got a copy of the Criminal Code, and you find out how to get the staff paid. We'll go from there."*

*Dale had the imagination to bring such talents aboard as O. Otto Moore, retired Colorado Supreme Court Chief Justice. Judge Moore was a fount of wisdom and a constant help to the rest of the staff.*

*Dale's infectious enthusiasm and drive, his availability through an almost always open door, and his positive approach to everything permeated the Denver D.A.'s Office for more than 10 years. That same cheerful determination transferred to almost the entire staff. Imagine a staff that actually looked forward to staff meetings, training dinners and office retreats!*

— **Velma Andrews**

The campaign in 1972 for Denver district attorney was a complicated one. John A. Dee, a former cabinet member of Mayor Currigan and former Notre Dame basketball coach, announced his candidacy for district attorney as an independent, even though he was a well-known Democrat. In addition, the office was not vacant. Incumbent Jarvis Seccombe had been conducting the office in a responsible manner. Finally, there was the national ticket; 1972 was a presidential election year, and George McGovern would be heading the Democratic party ticket against incumbent President Richard M. Nixon. It turned out that McGovern lost Denver by a tremendous margin, approximately 2 to 1.

My day-to-day campaign manager was Peter McLaughlin, who was creative and consistent. As is often the case in campaigns, the turning point was unforeseen. Jim Visser, a private investigator, along with a friend, brought to me information that there was a widespread practice of rolling back odometers on used cars before they were placed on automobile lots for resale. This issue seemed minor compared to the priorities I had announced: violent crime, organized crime, public corruption, white collar crime, career criminals, home burglaries, juvenile crime and drugs—particularly drug pushers. Nevertheless, the issue took hold, because it seemed that almost everyone had purchased a used car with a rolled-back odometer.

Seccombe's response was defensive and it did not set well with the voters. We won with a 33,000 vote margin of victory over Seccombe. Dee ran a poor third, but was a graceful loser. Rarely had an incumbent district attorney been defeated, but it happened this time and we prepared to assume office.

My basic philosophy was that the District Attorney's Office is a high public trust, and in fact one of the most powerful and important offices in Colorado. The thousands of decisions made each year are largely unreviewable, and a sense of fairness and justice is the bottom line. I recruited a top-notch staff and changed the previous practice of having, on average, a complete turnover of lawyers every two years. When I left office, the average prosecutor had seven years' experience. We delegated authority broadly, even when it sometimes resulted in embarrassment. Almost always the result was a more professional staff and a better quality of justice and crime control.

We recruited approximately 30 high-quality women who shared jobs with one another. This innovation has since spread. It brought a quality of support to the District Attorney's Office which had been absent in previous administrations. In addition, we recruited a cadre of skilled investigators to prepare cases with as much or more skill than the defense. It was a new approach to conducting the office.

It was an open office, and my telephone was listed during all 10 years in office. The office was used as a focal point to reform the system. We drafted and caused to be passed more than 100 significant pieces of legislation, losing only about half a dozen in a 10-year process. We more than doubled the number of trials with approximately the same number of lawyers as before, and we paid them much better through legislation we got enacted and appropriations we secured from the city. We made some mistakes, but hopefully had the good judgment to admit them. In fact, the best description of our approach to the office is presented next, in the form of a memorandum which I wrote to my successor before he was even named, but after I had announced my planned resignation as district attorney to run for Mayor in 1983.

Those 10 action-filled years involve many facets and experiences and tell much about the development of Denver and the judicial system in those years.

## Chapter 10

# The Best Prosecution Was An Acquittal

The case which I prosecuted the best resulted in an acquittal. It was an emotion-charged murder case which had to be tried, and which turned into a classic courtroom chess game.

The facts, though hotly contested, were not complicated. In the winter of 1979, the American embassy in Tehran had just been overrun and the embassy staff taken hostage. In the days following the takeover, emotions in this country ran high. A dozen young men in Southwest Denver, mostly teenagers, set out one evening to "hassle some Iranians" because of the embassy seizure. As they piled into several cars, some of them grabbed baseball bats.

They first went to the campus of Loretto Heights College, looking for some of the Iranian exchange students they knew attended that school. Finding none, they went to an apartment complex on Federal Boulevard and found a name on one of the mailboxes which they believed (correctly, as it turned out) to be Iranian—Afshin Shariati. Paul Moritsky, an athletic young high school student, and another teenager went to Shariati's second-floor apartment, smashed a window with their baseball bats and dashed away to one of the waiting cars. Shariati grabbed his deer rifle, ran to a second-floor balcony overlooking Federal Boulevard, aimed and fired, and then aimed and fired again. His two shots struck three of the young men, seriously wounding one and instantly killing Paul Moritsky. In those few seconds, a human tragedy occurred and an international incident erupted.

It was clear that what the young men did was wrong. Colorado law permits use of deadly force in response to an attempted bombing or arson, or in self-defense or in defense of others. Otherwise, killing a fleeing intruder is a crime. The theory of the law is that use of deadly force is justified to defend life, but not property.

We knew this was a concept with which many citizens disagreed. My wife felt that Shariati would certainly be acquitted, and I knew it was a likely prospect. But both the law and the circumstances required that a murder case be tried. After all, one young man was dead and another crippled.

From Washington, the Attorney General of the United States called Colorado Governor Richard Lamm about the case.

At that point, all of us were concerned about additional attacks by or against Iranians living in Denver. Since some felt that the Shariati case might become a factor in negotiations to free the American hostages, I decided to handle the case personally, along with Chuck Lepley, a chief deputy known for his careful preparation. The defense retained Walter Gerash and his associate, Scott Robinson. Gerash was an experienced, outspoken trial lawyer with whom I had played chess several times, and lost. We both knew this trial would be a chess game.

Gerash's first move was to file a series of pretrial motions. They were for the most part denied by the affable and hardworking trial judge, Daniel Sparr. One important defense motion was granted. The motion for a continuance resulted in the case being set for trial just a few weeks before Christmas, a full year after the shooting.

Because the community was so divided over the case, picking the jury took on added importance. The jury selection took a full week. To relieve the boredom and to make the points that our law applies, not Shariati's, and that the misconduct of the young men did not warrant killing, I asked one prospective juror:

"Tell me what you think about the adage, 'when in Rome, do as the Romans do'."

"Objection!" roared Gerash. "He's trying to give her a verbal Rorschach test."

"Denied," said the judge.

After her answer, I asked, "What is your reaction to the old saying, 'two wrongs don't make a right'?"

"Objection again, your honor," Gerash said as he jumped to his feet. "The law applies, not proverbs."

The judge again denied his objection. Most mornings before the trial resumed, Gerash and I would trade proverbs.

Gerash did a good job in questioning the prospective jurors, in one case discovering that a potential juror had been involved in a similar shooting years earlier. The end result was a jury with which both sides were well pleased.

We knew Gerash would do his best to broaden the scope of the trial, and to make it a trial of the backgrounds of our witnesses who had accompanied Paul Moritsky that fateful night. We made the next move, a motion to restrict such testimony.

"This is a murder case," I argued. "We shouldn't let the sideshow take over the circus."

The judge limited the scope of the testimony he would allow, but did rule that the defense could get into the cases we had filed against the young men for their conduct that night. However, during the pretrial hearing, we put on the stand Judge Dana Wakefield (a blind judge who had been a chief deputy in my office and who had filed these very cases while still in the District Attorney's Office). His powerful testimony, which Judge Sparr ruled could be used at trial if Gerash got into the other cases, caused Gerash to abandon that strategy. In effect, it was a checkmate for the prosecution.

The next strategic issue was the defendant's eyesight and how well he could see when he fired the fatal shots from the second floor balcony. The defense wanted to put into testimony an expert's opinion that Shariati had some impairment of his night vision. This would be a key issue in the case. We objected to the testimony unless Shariati submitted to an examination by our expert, the highly regarded head of the Opthalmology Department at the University of Colorado Health Sciences Center. The evidence on both sides was checkmated. Shariati did not submit to the test and the defense could not offer its expert testimony.

The strategic maneuvering continued with our motion requesting a night jury visit to the shooting scene. Gerash vigorously opposed the motion. Before making his ruling, the judge decided he would join counsel for both sides at the scene one night. We all met at a doughnut shop, then proceeded to the scene. Before we left, assistants from both sides arrived separately to begin conducting night reenactments of the balcony shooting.

Our reenactment showed that the night visibility was excellent. Gerash contended that his tests showed just the opposite. For his part, the judge was reluctant about a night trip by the jury to the scene, and he worried aloud about having the case decided by experts recounting reenactments. Using his broad discretion in deciding such issues, he ruled that the jury would be allowed to visit the scene during the daytime, and that reenactment evidence would not be allowed. Again, the defense and the prosecution had checkmated one another. "Interesting ploys," commented Gerash.

The defense was startled as we were cross-examining Shariati's American wife. On the night of the shooting, FBI Agent William Matens had taken a statement from Mrs. Shariati in which she quoted her husband as having said, as he returned from the balcony, that he had "hit two of them." A copy of Matens' report had been furnished to Gerash before the trial, but apparently he had missed it in the mass of pretrial documents which we had delivered to him. The statement was critical, because it undercut the defense theory that Shariati thought a bomb had been thrown into his apartment and that he had fired blindly into the night.

Gerash drew on his long experience in attempting to block admission of the statement. He knew that the FBI almost never would reveal its complete, original file, least of all in a state court. The judge agreed that the evidence would not be admitted unless the FBI's file was made fully available. When the FBI produced only part of the file, Judge Sparr chastised the agent who produced it and stormed from the bench. Our time was running short. Only my acquaintance with and calls to the head of the Criminal Division of the Justice Department in Washington allowed us to have the full FBI documents produced.

We completed our cross-examination of Mrs. Shariati and put Agent Matens on the stand. The jury heard all of that evidence. While it was a great strategic victory, it ultimately was not enough to overcome the fact that the shooting was in response to an unprovoked baseball bat attack on Shariati's home.

The last chess move came as we began closing arguments. The trial had taken several weeks, and we knew that the closing arguments would be more important than in most cases. We had analyzed Gerash's approach in previous trials. He was at his best counter-punching, building his argument around the prosecution's opening argument. (The prosecution argues first, then the defense, and then the prosecutor has the last word because the state has the burden of proof. The prosecution can waive its first argument, but if the defense then chooses to make no argument, there is nothing to rebut and the case goes to the jury on the evidence and the judge's instructions, alone.)

We gambled that, in so important a case, Gerash could not resist making a closing argument.

"Your Honor, the People will waive their closing argument and are prepared to have the case submitted to the jury at this time on the evidence and your instructions. Of course, if Mr. Gerash should choose to make a closing argument, we would in that event exercise our right to respond," I stated when the judge called on me for our closing argument.

Gerash was surprised. He told the court he needed a few moments to get his thoughts together, and then made a good argument—but not as good as it might otherwise have been.

The long trial over, the case went to the jury on a Friday afternoon. Late Saturday, the jury reached a verdict of not guilty.

There is an old saying that the prosecution never loses, because its duty is to seek justice, not merely to convict. The Shariati case is a classic example of that doctrine. It was a courtroom chess game in a tournament which had to be held. It also proved again that my wife's predictions about case outcomes are uncannily correct.

## Chapter 11

# "You've Got My Attention"

The story is that a sheriff in Longview, Texas, tired of not getting his cut from an illegal poker game and ran the Texas Mafia out of town. For whatever reason, Norman Granberry and his brother, Archie, along with Ted Bullard and their colleagues, came to Denver in the 60's. By the time I took office, they controlled almost two dozen topless bars and other establishments. Complaints were received constantly of their swindling of customers, assaulting of prostitutes and a range of other illegal activities.

The Texans' bars were distinguished by what was called on the streets a champagne bust-out operation. Cheap bottles of champagne were sold by shapely "hostesses" for $50 a bottle. Our grand jury was particularly shocked upon hearing that the hostesses used what are called "spit glasses." They would spit their champagne back into these glasses. This served two purposes. The bottles of champagne were consumed faster. And, the used champagne from the spit glasses was rebottled and resold at $50 a bottle.

It was not uncommon for a customer to pay out $1,000 or more in a single night. Sex was offered, and sometimes furnished, as part of the operation. Some of these establishments "ran" the customers' credit cards twice or more for each bottle purchased. At least one of the bars slipped knockout drops in a customer's glass before taking his wallet.

We began an investigation which eventually closed most of their establishments. Ted Bullard was tried and convicted on multiple counts of securities fraud. But Norman Granberry, an articulate, handsome leader of the organization, carefully kept distance between himself and his operatives.

The Texans' operations were obviously profitable, but theirs was not a class act. At the height of the investigation, a source within the Texans' organization told us that one of the suspects had been seeking out someone who would kill me for $500. The grand jury subpoenaed the suspect. He took the Fifth Amendment, but I sharply chastised him both for his criminal solicitations and his cheapness. Five hundred dollars was well below the market price for contract murder.

During an investigation of the Denver Building Department, Norman Granberry was implicated in bribery of Building Department officials. The grand jury indicted, and we convicted, 11 people in the course of the investigation. The twelfth person indicted was Norman Granberry. He was charged with paying a $5,000 cash bribe to the Building Department supervisor.

Because of the extensive publicity, the case was moved to Craig, a town in northwestern Colorado. The flight to Craig on Rocky Mountain Airways looked like something from an Agatha Christie novel. The only other passengers were Jim Visser, my investigator; Norman Granberry; his chief defense attorney, Alex Keller (a Denver trial lawyer with an excellent reputation); his assistant, Robert Johnson; and several of Granberry's men. "We're safer all being on the same plane," Visser remarked.

The trial went smoothly. The bribe-takers we had convicted told of Granberry's $5,000 payment. It would have been better if our witnesses had been Boy Scouts, but you take them as you find them.

Granberry took the stand in his own defense. He freely admitted paying the bribe. His defense was that the Building Department officials extorted the payment from him, and that if he had not paid up, his construction project would have been stopped. There was some merit in that concern.

While the jury was deliberating Granberry's fate, he repeatedly said to us, "You've got my attention. You've got my attention." The jury agreed with his extortion defense and found him not guilty. But not long after that trial, Granberry converted his main topless bar, called Tricky Dicky's, into a standard country and western bar. It looked like Granberry was actually going straight. We remained skeptical.

Late one night, Granberry was returning to his Clayton Street residence after having closed out an establishment for the night. As he walked up his front steps he was stopped by a gunman, later identified as Charles Workman. Workman, we learned later, had been hired by one of the Texans to kill Granberry.

He robbed Granberry and shot him in the head. The gun must have been defective, because while the bullet lodged in Granberry's skull, the head wound was not serious. When the police response to the scene was unsatisfactory, Granberry angrily drove himself to the emergency room of a private hospital where the bullet was removed; but, the wound to his pride remained.

He began his own investigation while we conducted ours. I had persuaded Workman to confess (for which he received a 25-year sentence), and we began working up the chain to the person who had planned the shooting. In the meantime, Granberry began with the person he thought planned the attack. Both paths led to Larry Goetz, a member of the loosely organized Texas Mafia, who had the Clown's Den bar in downtown Denver.

One afternoon Granberry and his lawyer, Keller, came to my office, played a tape recording of a conversation with Goetz, which was somewhat corroborative of Goetz' involvement, and offered to help in the investigation. Granberry proposed a most unusual plan, which we accepted with some modifications. We would "kidnap" Granberry, let the word out on the street that he had been killed, and see what Goetz said and did. We modified the plan by having ace undercover investigator Kenneth Patrick Brown of the Colorado Bureau of Investigation meet first with Goetz.

True to form, Goetz offered to pay Brown for killing Granberry. In broad daylight on Seventeenth Street, Granberry was abducted into a rented black limousine. We hid him out for several nights in Greeley, Cheyenne and Boulder, while the criminal grapevine on the street buzzed about Granberry's abduction. Brown, wearing his customary body microphone, then called on Goetz and delivered to him Granberry's wallet and ring. Goetz paid Brown for the "murder," made incriminating statements on the tape, and was promptly arrested.

Goetz was tried, convicted of conspiracy to commit murder and sentenced to the state penitentiary. With that conviction, the violence surrounding the Texas Mafia ended. A few more convictions and bar closings followed, but the back of the Texas Mafia, which Granberry helped bring to Denver, was broken. It was done through the plan which Granberry himself had proposed. After Goetz was sentenced, Granberry again said, "As I told you, you've got my attention."

## Chapter 12

# The Nature of Crime and Criminals

**Observation 1. Swindlers**

Swindlers are inherently likeable. They are great salesmen. Almost without exception they would have been excellent politicians, except they chose a calling which is often more lucrative. Even after spending weeks in a courtroom with the mission of convicting the swindler, you hear the jury's verdict with mixed emotion, because you have developed a grudging admiration for the defendant's misdirected skills.

Bill Riley is a case in point. Founder of one of the largest real estate enterprises in Colorado history, he was a combination of Glen Turner (of Dare to be Great fame), John M. King (convicted head of King Resources) and auto industry wizard Lee Iacocca.

After the 1982 Denver Grand Jury indicted Riley, it took half a year to apprehend him. Along with the combined efforts of my investigators, the FBI, Interpol (the international police network), the U.S. State Department, Chilean authorities, police agencies in Ohio, Arizona and Florida, postal inspectors, hundreds of wanted posters—and some luck—played roles. Only Riley can tell how he slipped through an Interpol surveillance ring, left a hotel in Santiago and managed to slip by U.S. Customs in Florida.

When we finally got him into court, he was gracious and upbeat. As was my custom with all the defendants I personally prosecuted, I shook hands with him in an anteroom at his first court date. His grasp was firm, even though his hands were manacled in front of him. He became visibly distraught only when I could not recall what he described as our chance meeting on a ski slope several years earlier.

From the outset, Riley made it known that he wanted a trial separate from his four lieutenants. He got his way by hiding out in Florida under an assumed name. When I told his lawyer I took a dim view of his using an Irish alias (Gregory O'Brien), he took another alias. He was arrested by the FBI as he was closing yet another real estate deal in Florida. His arrest came just hours after a Denver jury began deliberating the fate of Richard Heller, Paul Bragar and Tom Thornton, his top colleagues in Income Mortgage and Realty, Inc. After they were found guilty (joining Steve Swanson, who pleaded guilty earlier), Riley asked for a change of venue because of the extensive publicity surrounding both that trial and our international manhunt for Riley and his assets.

Judge Warren Martin, one of Colorado's premiere trial judges, said from the bench, "Mr. Tooley, how would you like to try this case in La Junta in August?" "That, your Honor, would be cruel and unusual punishment," I replied, knowing how hot La Junta would be in August. Understandably, irate phone calls from La Junta taught me to make no similar comment when the judge announced that the case would be tried in Gunnison.

Changes of venue rarely accomplish their intended purpose. This case was no exception. At a lunch break during jury selection I asked a waitress in a Gunnison restaurant if she knew anything about the Bill Riley case. "No," she said, "until we heard it was coming to Gunnison. Then everybody began studying up on it."

Like most skilled swindlers, Bill Riley had written the script. He had his separate trial, an excellent and knowledgeable defense lawyer in Joseph Davies, and a trial 200 miles from Denver. Most of the witnesses against him were the same ones who had testified against his co-defendants in the Denver trial several months earlier, and he had complete transcripts of their testimony.

Swindlers think ahead and set the trial stage far better than do other defendants, but they have one predictable weakness. They believe they can be as persuasive with a jury as they were with investors in their schemes.

Bill Riley, like countless swindlers before him, took the stand in his own defense. He broke down in tears precisely 45 minutes into his testimony. He choked up when it was time for the noon recess. He hugged his attractive wife just when the jury entered the courtroom. He remembered the dates, content and exhibit numbers of hundreds of pages of documents. He used the same articulate style which had never failed him in hundreds of radio programs and presentations to potential victims.

The difference—one which swindlers never fully understand—is that the jury has already heard scores of victims whose testimony sharply contradicts the swindler's in-court sales pitch. On the witness stand a swindler is forced to say that all of his victims testified falsely and that he alone is telling the truth.

Even after a full day on the witness stand, Riley's remarkable buoyancy remained. Our greetings each morning in court were always courteous. In a small town during the long trial, litigants simply can't avoid running into one another. All those chance encounters were equally civil. The only angry exchange came during my final series of questions on cross-examination—and even that I believe he had planned, undoubtedly to the chagrin of his lawyer. Even during times of high stress, swindlers remain friendly, optimistic, articulate, controlled—and greedy.

Because of the complexity of the case, the jurors were permitted to take notes. After the closing arguments, they spent seven hours reviewing their notes and the evidence before finding Riley guilty on multiple counts of securities fraud.

There is always an electric tension in the courtroom when the jury's verdict is about to be read. While there is a professional satisfaction in convicting a swindler, there is no joy in it—particularly when the defendant's family is seated faithfully only a few feet away and you know the shock and pain they are experiencing. But that is matched many times over by the pain and loss which hundreds of victims received at the swindler's hands.

In the state penitentiary at Canon City, where Riley was sent to serve his sentence, his buoyancy remained. Fellow inmates at the Denver County Jail had nicknamed Riley the Six Million Dollar Man (referring to the $6 million that investors lost in his bond scheme). Swindlers enjoy respect in prison from both fellow inmates and staff. The first diagnostic report from the penitentiary described Riley as a very good inmate, although "somewhat manipulative." Sources at the prison say he became an effective motivational teacher there.

Bill Riley is not unique in Denver history. He joins a long line of prominent swindlers who thought they could overpower the system—Fred Ward, John M. King, Juan Cortez and Dr.

Sandra Brown, to name only a few. All were likeable, intelligent, optimistic—and greedy. All left guillible victims and human tragedy in their wakes. But all of them were brought to justice.

No one wins in a criminal case, except the public and those thousands of citizens who may never be victims because of the deterrence to would-be swindlers from such cases.

*EDITOR'S NOTE: On November 18, 1985 (subsequent, of course, to Dale Tooley's death) the Colorado Supreme Court overturned the conviction of William G. Riley. However, in a separate case Riley had pleaded guilty to felony theft, and had served a sentence for that offense concurrently with the one given him for the fraud conviction which was overturned.*

## Observation 2. A Tale of Two Crooks

From all outward appearances, Juan Francisco Cortez and Dr. Sandra Brown had little in common. Cortez was not well educated. He has been kicked out of the San Antonio Police Department for abuse of force and came to Denver only because he managed to marry the daughter of a Denver millionaire.

Sandra Brown, by contrast, was a Ph.D., commonly addressed as "Doctor Brown." She was a well-known Eastern businesswoman who was the first woman in the country to have received a Small Business Investment Company license from the federal government. She was appointed by President Nixon to serve on a presidential advisory commission, and had served as president and director of scores of companies. She visited Denver because she had just taken over control of the multimillion dollar Holiday Gifts Company, a nationally known mail order firm headquartered in the Denver area.

Cortez had a long history of involvement in illegal schemes, including phony coal mine deals in Alabama, timber scams in Central America and Swiss financial manipulations. By contrast, Brown had developed a reputation of being able to rescue troubled companies, although her cash flow practices sometimes raised bankers' eyebrows and caused them to close out her accounts.

Actually, Cortez and Brown were made from the same mold: intelligent, persuasive and willing to do or say almost anything to make money. Their ends justified their means. Their activities in Denver resulted in both of them going to prison for felony theft by deception. Brown was a check kiting artist and Cortez a con game wizard. They had one more thing in common. Both had the misfortune to have their cases assigned to and investigated by Doyle Marshall, a retired postal inspector with a national reputation whom I appointed as my chief investigator.

### Dr. Sandra Brown

Charles Goldberg, a prominent Denver lawyer and former judge, called on me in his capacity as counsel for Cherry Creek National Bank. "My client has been swindled out of $1.3 million through an interstate check kiting operation run by a shrewd woman named Dr. Sandra Brown," Goldberg said. "The U.S. Attorney says it is simply a dispute between two banks, and refuses to prosecute. We are asking that you bring this woman to justice."

Our preliminary review backed up everything Goldberg said. Brown had written more than $36 million in checks on her accounts at Cherry Creek National and at Bank Hapoalim, an Israeli-owned bank located in New York City. She took advantage of the five to seven days it took for checks drawn on her account in New York to clear when deposited in Denver, and vice versa. Because she received immediate credit when the deposits were made, she had a huge "float" to spend. The float belonged not to her, but to the banks, but she spent $1.3 million of it before her house of cards was discovered and collapsed.

This was one of the crimes which is so complicated to unravel and which involves so many thousands of documents that prosecutors are often reluctant to proceed. Yet failure to prosecute would mean a double standard of justice, where the big time crooks go free and the garden variety thieves go to jail. I decided that we would file the case and that I would try it, along with Chief Deputy Steve Marsters.

Dr. Brown was an engaging woman who looked younger than her 41 years. She believed she could easily persuade men, but was less sure about women. On the day of trial, when the case was transferred from a woman judge to the courtroom of Judge Joseph Quinn (now a justice of the Colorado Supreme Court), she quickly waived the jury and we tried the case to the court. Her lawyer, Anthony Renzo, prepared her well. She might have won an acquittal, except for the reams of her own daily, incriminating notes which were uncovered by Investigator Marshall as he meticulously questioned her former associates.

Trial lawyers tend to blame losses on the witnesses and credit victories to their own persuasiveness. In fact, the quality of the investigation has more to do with each result. Marshall had prepared well and the evidence was introduced effectively. Visual aids (slides and charts) helped to simplify the facts. Dr. Brown wrongly thought she could fast-talk the judge. She was found guilty and was sentenced to prison for 4½ years. She is a remarkable woman who could have gone far in business had she only developed a proper code of conduct and the willpower to reject illegal means.

### Juan Francisco Cortez

Cortez had the same potential, and same absence of a code of conduct. One afternoon, I received a call from a Denver detective. He asked that we come to his house to look at some strange records of a man named Juan Cortez. The detective's wife had a girl friend who had left the records with her. The friend proved to be Cortez' new wife, and we obtained a search warrant for the records. Thus began the strange saga of Juan Cortez.

The records disclosed a long history of use of phony certificates of deposit and loan commitments, as devices to separate victims from their money and property. About the same time the detective called, we began receiving calls about a con man named Cortez. He had set up shop in the fabulous estate of his new in-laws, a place called Utopia. He told prospective victims that his in-laws were the hired help, and that he was buying the place. Using that elegant setting, complete with golf course, glass-topped swimming pool under the house, moat and geese on the grounds, he seemed legitimate. He fast-talked a string of victims out of money, half an airplane company, interests in oil and gas properties, and even a 50% interest in Wyoming mineral interests which one witness valued at in excess of one billion dollars. Cortez himself never paid for anything. He managed to have his victims pay for all meals, hotel expenses, airplane tickets and even got what he called "walking around money" from them.

The complexity of the investigation matched that of Cortez' scheme. We used body microphones, search warrants and witnesses from throughout North America before we arrested him. He quickly retained Phillip Lowery, one of Denver's best trial lawyers. True to form, he even swindled Lowery out of his fee for the long trial. Lowery may yet have an interest in Cortez' proposed book and movie, "The World's Greatest Entrepreneur."

The long trial was a pleasure to try with Jeffrey Bayless, a chief deputy in our Complex Prosecutions Unit. Cortez testified for a full day. As I questioned him on the stand, more than 50 times he was forced to contradict the sworn testimony of prior witnesses. Although the jury returned verdicts of guilty, one of the jurors said later that the case had reached the outer edge of complexity which a jury of ordinary citizens could be expected to understand.

As is unfortunately the case in most convictions, Cortez was given an appeal bond. We knew he would resume his illegal ways, and within a month had evidence of it. In short order, he stole half interest in a house and a part interest in a blind man's concert piano. With that, the judge revoked his bond and ordered him to begin serving his 5½- to 13-year sentence.

A line from a play says, "If you steal something small, you go to jail. If you steal something big, you'll get an award some day." While that is too often true, it was not true in the cases of Brown and Cortez. The real bottom line benefit from the massive commitment of time and resources to these cases is this message to the public and to would-be criminals: The law is applied equally. Crooks go to prison. No one is above the law.

### Observation 3. Violence

Most citizens have little appreciation of the nature and level of violence in our society, because they see so little of it first-hand. Criminals who commit crimes of violence and the police who combat them daily don't understand the true dimensions of violence either, because they see so much of it. For the most part, violence is a media event to most citizens and an expected, inevitable way of life to criminals and the police.

Over a decade we worked closely with more than a dozen grand juries. Almost without exception, by the end of their year of service they had transformed their own views of violence as they learned for the first time of a criminal way of life in their own city.

A good illustration of all of this is the case of Peter Schamber. He was the career criminal who hired Charles Workman to kill a reputed member of the Texas Mafia, but Workman only wounded his target. Before he was convicted and sentenced to the penitentiary he disclosed Schamber's role. Schamber, in turn, provided the grand jury with critical, detailed evidence of a series of murders and other high crimes. The grand jurors were shocked at the scope and casualness of these crimes.

**Observation 4. Guns**

With more than 100 million guns at large in our country, and no realistic way to limit their availability, widespread use of firearms should come as no surprise. In some subcultures, a person is not fully dressed without his "heater" (firearm).

During my first term, we organized a series of raids on after-hours clubs and closed them as public nuisances. In one such raid in the 3000 block on Downing Street, we heard a great deal of metal banging as we entered the building. I thought the noise must be from a defective air conditioning system. Just then a detective held up a box full of guns—guns which patrons had dropped on the floor as we entered. Predictably, none of the patrons admitted to having ever owned or seen any of the weapons.

Many police officers regularly carry two handguns, even while off duty. Even some reporters are unaware of this practice. One day a television reporter called seeking our approval of a "staged" armed robbery to be conducted at a Denver bar to demonstrate the variances in eyewitness testimony. We vetoed the plan as exceptionally dangerous, particularly when the reporter said it was to be done at Copperfield's. Copperfield's is a popular establishment on Colfax near the Police Administration Building, and is regularly frequented by police officers. Any person even posing as an armed robber there would have looked like a Swiss cheese in a matter of seconds.

Persons not carrying firearms can sometimes acquire them very quickly. Several years ago, an unwise man played the jukebox in a bar during a televised Denver Broncos football game. An angry viewer drove home, got his gun, returned and shot and killed the jukebox fan. We correctly charged the killer with first degree murder. Despite the obvious evidence of deliberation, the jury returned a verdict of guilty only to second degree murder. It seems that the citizens on the jury saw some measure of justification in killing a person so callous as to interrupt a televised Denver Broncos game against the Colts.

## Observation 5. Threats of Violence

It is ironic that some groups opposed to violence are willing themselves to threaten use of violence. A movie called "Snuff" was to be shown at a Denver drive-in theater. The movie reportedly filmed the actual death and dismemberment of two young Argentine prostitutes. When the scheduled showing became known, a group of women who opposed violence against women threatened to burn down the drive-in theater if the film were shown there. We persuaded the owner to withdraw the film if it were rejected by a panel we would organize to screen the movie. The panel included such diverse members as an ex-Marine prosecutor (whose last movie was Bambi), and a free spirit who thought anything should be freely shown. The panel was unanimously repulsed at the sickness of the filmed dismemberment of the young women, and opposed the showing; the owner kept the film out of Denver, and the women didn't burn down the theater.

Threats of violence against the system and the district attorney in a major city come with the territory. Fortunately, they are generally made by people who are drunk, are only temporarily angry or who couldn't succeed even if they tried.

We once received a call saying that a bomb was about to go off at an evening session of a grand jury then in progress in the City and County Building. We quickly evacuated the grand jury from the courtroom, but found no bomb. Meanwhile, a bomb went off at the Federal Courthouse several blocks away. Those bombers clearly knew nothing of our structure of government.

Some violence-prone people do maintain a degree of class. At 5 one morning I was awakened at home by a caller who said he was going to kill me. "We have four children. We don't get up around here until 7. Why would you make this threat at such an ungodly hour?" I asked. Without hesitation the caller said, "I'm terribly sorry. It was inconsiderate of me. You see, I don't have a telephone easily available at my job.

### Observation 6. A Violence Saturation Point

There is a certain unreality surrounding violence. I have been at more death scenes, seen more abused children, viewed more photographs of bodies and injuries, and talked with more victims and their survivors than I want to recall. But it was not until my last year in office that I experienced that saturation point which causes some police officers and prosecutors abruptly to change careers.

My own saturation point was reached as I tried Dr. James Franklin for manslaughter and criminal abortion in the tragic killing of a young mother. During a botched office abortion, the doctor had macerated the fetus, failed to complete the abortion, and sent the young woman home to a certain death from infection. The dying mother was found by her four-year-old son. Both the testimony at the trial and the photographs were so vivid that they interfered with sleep, even after the jury found the doctor guilty as charged.

Constant exposure to violence requires that a person establish defense mechanisms to deal with it. The irony—and perhaps the saving grace—is that even those defense mechanisms have their saturation point. Perhaps our society would be healthier and safer if citizens better understood the nature and extent of violence, and if criminals and police officers did not so readily accept it as an inevitable way of life.

### Observation 7. Drugs

We may never know the full extent of the huge price our country still pays because of the drug culture which grew up during the Viet Nam era of the 60's.

Because of the sudden explosion of drug use, there is a generation gap in understanding about drugs. Those under thirty are much more knowledgeable about drugs than those over forty. An older woman from northwest Denver once described a group of young people sharing a joint. "Young people are so generous," she marveled. "I saw four young men downtown who were so poor they were sharing the same cigarette."

In deciding at what level a criminal case should be concluded, prosecutors customarily consider two main factors, the nature of the crime and the background of the defendant. In drug cases, it is often hard to know if the defendant is a pusher or merely a user (because most pushers use and many users push), if he is an addict who occasionally steals, or a burglar who occasionally uses, and if the defendant's drug involvement is an aberration or a habit.

One day a patient called to report that she did not receive the drugs prescribed for her while she was in a Denver hospital. This complaint became frequent, and a special team of narcotics officers began an investigation. About that time, a private hospital reported that a nurse had slit with a razor blade a syringe containing morphine prescribed for a terminal cancer patient. The nurse had then substituted water for the morphine. Audits of hospital drug lockers showed unexplained shortages. In one hospital, a common joke was that one of the nurses was "perking on Percodan." Some nurses came forward to confess. Others sought treatment for drug abuse.

Almost all of these nurses had otherwise spotless records, yet they had violated both the criminal laws and their professional responsibilities, sometimes endangering their patients in the process. These were classic examples of serious crimes committed by otherwise good people who would be unlikely to repeat their crimes.

How should they be handled? I decided we should err on the side of society and require a plea to a felony or trial, but that we would not oppose probation. That decision was controversial. Perhaps it was too harsh for the defendants, but not for society or for the untold number of victims who suffered pain needlessly because of these crimes. These cases and their handling seemed to have a rapid deterrent effect on the problem.

One has to be living in a cave not to know that a majority of high school and college students have at least tried marijuana. It is big business. Prosecutors in the Florida area report that it is so profitable that drug dealers often sell the marijuana shipment for a negotiated price, then "throw in" the container. The container may be a boat, a truck, or even a four-engine airplane. Alaska has even made it legal to cultivate marijuana for personal use. Many other states, like Colorado, have removed jail penalties for private possession of small amounts.

Two things are certain: marijuana is not good for you, but it is clearly not as bad as heroin, the amphetamines and other hard drugs. I have had endless discussions with young people who argue that alcohol is more damaging than marijuana. To one group I said, "That is irrelevant. That is like saying theft is okay because rape is so much worse."

We should not lock people up for possession of small amounts of marijuana. On the other hand, to legalize marijuana or other drugs will inevitably expand the number of people exposed to the illicit drug distribution network. It is a matter of balance, which our present policies are generally achieving.

Cocaine is the prestige, expensive drug of the middle and upper classes. It does not have the *physical* addicting qualities of heroin. However, experiments with monkeys and other evidence have shown cocaine to be more reinforcing of continued use than heroin.

A shocking thing with cocaine, and some other drugs, is the price markup. We prosecuted a case involving several kilos of particularly pure cocaine. After the trial was over and the defendants sentenced, I instructed the police not to destroy the drugs, which would have been the usual practice. Since the street value of this cocaine was several hundred thousand dollars, I reasoned that it should be of substantial value to a pharmaceutical company engaged in manufacturing medicines used to treat the eye disease glaucoma.

I called the head of a major drug company and asked if his firm would be interested in purchasing the cocaine. He said they would be very interested and suggested that we begin the complicated process of securing federal approval for the transfer. It seemed impolitic to discuss price in that first conversation, but I had visions of so high a price that both drug enforcement and drug treatment programs could be supported from the proceeds. A week later I talked with him again.

"What is the fair market value for this quality of cocaine?" I asked politely.

"We'll pay $2,500 for it, lock, stock and barrel," he replied.

When I pointed out the huge difference between that and its illicit street value, he said simply that "there is a big markup on the street." The work and red tape of securing the transfer approval would have cost more than $2,500, so we had the cocaine destroyed, after all.

Stopping cocaine traffic will continue to be difficult for

several reasons. First, it is compact. An easily concealed quantity can sell for tens of thousands of dollars. We once prosecuted a cocaine pusher who transported cocaine from his South American source concealed in his hollowed-out skis. Second, the distribution network and the users are generally a much different group than heroin pushers and other drug dealers. Narcotics detectives do not have the same sources of information within this new, often affluent strata of society. Third, there is a widely-held belief that cocaine use may be no worse than marijuana use, and that it should be treated the same. People with that view have not seen how often violence is generated out of the big dollar cocaine transactions.

At least in Denver, heroin use seems to be on the decline. By 1983, the average purity of street heroin in Denver fell to an all-time low. There are several reasons.

Young people are increasingly aware that heroin is a killer drug. Narcotics detectives have good sources of information, even when the major opium sources shifted from Southeast Asia (the Golden Triangle) to Southwest Asia (the Golden Crescent) and Mexico. And, some of the treatment programs seem to have had a long range, positive impact. Thousands of Viet Nam veterans who used heroin overseas abruptly ended their use when they returned home. This "cold turkey" withdrawal from heroin gave new hope to drug free treatment programs. Medical research into addiction is on the verge of coming up with a chemical, similar to antibuse for alcoholics, which may help block heroin use.

There is no one answer or solution, but there are some lessons we should have learned. The generation gap in drug education should be closed. Most drug education materials are produced by those over forty for consumption by those under twenty. Drug enforcement should focus even more on hard drugs and pushers. Our resources are limited. It is better to develop quality cases against the bigger fish, even if the cases are fewer in number, than more cases against the minnows. Greater flexibility in medical research and drug treatment is necessary to address the constantly changing drug scene. All of this might not win the war on drugs, but it would help contain it.

## Chapter 13

# A Memorandum To My Successor

*I was one of seven individuals who applied for Dale's job following his resignation, and each of us received copies of his "To My Successor" memo. In reading it, I heard the echoes of many conversations which Dale and I had during the past 10 years. Some of the messages were ones which I had used daily, others had been forgotten and still others were stored in the recesses of my mind.*

*However, seeing it all in one place in a capsulized form let me know that there was a constant link from Dale's administration to what turned out to be my administration—a link that extended beyond our personal and professional relationship.*

*Even though I am well familiar with the contents of the memo, I refer to it every now and then in order to test myself. While the memo has always had meaning for me, it obtains greater significance with every day that I serve in this job. The tradition lives on!*

— **Norm Early**

In November of 1982 I announced my resignation as Denver district attorney. After announcing my resignation, I reflected on my decade of experience and dictated the following memorandum to my yet-to-be named successor:

**I am dictating this to you, even though I don't yet know who you are. Before you are appointed, I thought it might be valuable to you to have the benefit of what I have learned from experience as central stars on which to fix your own course. You may, of course, find these inapplicable to you or you may chart a different course. However, for whatever weight and benefit**

**you may give this, here are my ideas and advice.**

1. **Doing Justice: Setting the Tone.** Everyone knows that the district attorney's first obligation is to seek justice, and convictions are secondary to it. I have found it important to reiterate that in different ways in hundreds of thousands of conversations with the staff, the police and members of the public. Don't underestimate the importance of setting that tone and repeating it often. It is awfully easy in this business for people to take a cue from the district attorney and become over-zealous, unfair, unreasonable or vindictive. You simply can't assume that a policy once said is always remembered. You are the moral leader not only of the office, but of the criminal justice system and, in fact, in the minds of much of the public, of local government.

2. **Priorities.** It is easy to be diverted. I found it useful to remember often the priorities I established when I was first elected: crime prevention, violent crimes, career criminals, organized criminal activity, drugs (especially hard drugs and drug pushers), juvenile offenders, home burglaries, major swindles, rights of victims, and building public confidence in our system of justice. You ought to figure out what your priorities are going to be, review them regularly, and do your best to allocate resources along those lines.

3. **Make Decisions Without Fear or Favor.** There will be many decisions to be made where the popular and comfortable direction is easily seen. You can't help but be aware of that. However, it is essential that you and the staff call them as you see them. I always found it useful, for example, to tell every new deputy that he or she will undoubtedly be called upon by some lawyer or defendant or interested party, who will claim to be a close friend of mine or a supporter of mine in the last election. I told each deputy in advance to disregard any such comments; to treat the case like any other; and if anything, to bend toward trial rather than toward disposition whenever any such tactics are used or suggested. In ten years, I don't think I ever had

occasion to place on a file a direction that a case be handled in a particular way—except for policies such as how categories of cases ought to be dealt with. With our staff, I think you would properly have an in-house revolt if any effort were made to interfere with the handling of a case in the usual manner.

4. **Personnel.** From time to time, I have hired or promoted a staff member and been wrong in my judgment. Never, however, have I hired anyone believing that he or she would not be an excellent addition to the staff. You won't bat 1,000 percent, nobody does. From observing other offices, however, I am convinced that the quality of the staff is directly proportional to your resisting the tremendous pressures you will receive monthly to hire the relative or friend of a good friend or supporter. Set up a screening mechanism (I have successfully used Brooke Wunnicke's talents in this regard), both to save your time and to help in the recruitment of top-notch people. At the same time, talent is the stock in trade of the District Attorney's Office, and you should keep your eyes and ears open for good people. In this regard, special efforts have to be made to seek out and recruit the very best of minority deputies. Our office simply would be less effective if we had only a token Black, Chicano or woman representative. This takes a lot of effort, and this is one area where your own time has to be expended.

5. **Delegation of Authority and Responsibility.** When I took office, there was a very vertical decision-making process here. Perhaps that was necessary given the 50% per year turnover at that time. However, most District Attorney Offices still operate in that vertical mode. I urge you not to slip into that trap. You cannot recruit and retain quality people if they consider themselves clerks and nonprofessionals. Obviously, you have to set general policies, but you must delegate to the staff the right to be wrong in a given case. Occasionally, a new lawyer will ask me about office policies. I try to tell the new deputy that there are really only two major ones: no rule is so inflexible that if

followed it would achieve an unjust result; and if you do a good job, you get to keep it. Everything else really is a part of those two policies.

6. **Your Accessibility.** The staff and even the public come with great hesitation into the District Attorney's Office. I have found it important to keep that door almost always wide open. I have used everything from citizens' meetings, to citizens' call-ins, to radio programs, to advisory groups and task forces in order to maintain accessibility. If you don't do that, you are not going to have your finger on the pulse of the needs of the criminal justice system. Also, you will not be perceived as being the chief law officer of the city. I have found that a couple of speeches each week is about par for the course, and leaving plenty of time for questions keeps you on the ball. You may find other ways to maintain accessibility, but keep in mind that it is part and parcel of leadership.

7. **Seeking Reforms.** The criminal justice system has tremendous inertia. The district attorney's position is one of the very few which can initiate change—and even that is sometimes painfully slow. Take a broad view of your role—whether it is opposing casino gambling, advocating a change in the exclusionary rule, pushing for sentencing reform, designing neighborhood prevention efforts, or attempting to speed up the whole justice system. You can usually predict with some accuracy the amount of heat you will get in each effort. Don't try to dance too many dances at once. Sometimes, there will be battles which are important to be fought which you're pretty sure can't be won—such as reforming the bail bond system. As to those, you have to take a long-range view and recognize that change is coming and that you may have to go back to the well more than once to be successful. The worst thing to do is to lay back and assume that the system is operating at peak performance and that no other major changes are needed. The system calcifies itself. The district attorney is the one position with independence and clout to energize the system. You shouldn't

waste that capacity.

8. **Working With Reporters.** We have an increasingly active media in Denver, as you must know. I urge you not to muzzle the deputies. Most offices have rules which restrict or prohibit a deputy district attorney from talking to the press. Those rules don't work, because reporters will figure out a way to talk to the person who really has the facts. Such rules would cause friction and often inaccuracies. Encourage the deputies to know what they can and can't say, to tell the truth, or to say they can't talk about it. Avoid the temptation to hire a press secretary. The reporters won't trust the person in that position, and it will look political. I have almost never held press conferences and rarely have used press releases. Also, I have made it a practice of not calling the press. The reporters call every day to see what's going on, and I think there is a real responsibility to share what is, in fact, within the public's right to know. Whatever you say, someone will claim it is done for obscure political motivation. However, I think that criticism just goes with the territory and I know of no way of avoiding it. You are a member of the executive branch, not the judicial branch, the public has a right to know what we do, to the extent that the information will not adversely affect a person's rights, and if a mistake has been made, it's better to acknowledge it up front than to try to cover it up.

9. **Caesar's Wife.** Perhaps more than any other public office, the District Attorney's Office must be above reproach. I have all of the deputies and investigators fill out annual disclosure statements which are filed and which the press knows are available. (Interestingly enough, no reporter has ever asked to look at them, although I am sure they would be most interested if we said we had them and they were secret!) This approach helps remind the staff that it is not just a conflict, but the appearance of a conflict, which is to be avoided. Likewise, keep aware that there are certain places you simply should not go, nor should your

staff—such as Gaetano's (a reputed organized crime hangout), to an event where known criminals are going to be, or anywhere where you have reason in advance to know that someone will be violating the law—even if it is only someone smoking marijuana. I have personally made it a rule not to go to Las Vegas. That's an example of a place where the public is going to think something's improper, even if it isn't, if the district attorney is there. You may think this too restrictive, and perhaps it is, but the point is clear. Don't tolerate anything which compromises you or the office.

10. **Your Own Time.** I have found it impossible to conduct this office in less than 60 hours per week. You may be able to improve on that. However, you have to decide how you are going to spend your time. Try to manage by exception. Keep track of where you are spending your time so you can adjust it. I find that approximately one-fourth of my time is spent in administrative matters, one-fourth in dealing with the public and other agencies (broadly defined), one-fourth dealing in some manner with the Grand Jury, investigations or keeping abreast of what the office is or ought to be looking into, and the remaining one-fourth on cases which either I am handling or which I discuss with members of the staff. The amount of time you may spend actually trying cases could vary greatly from mine. I have tried to try a case personally about twice a year, but I find that they tend to be complicated ones (the last eight averaged two weeks each); and, if you are trying it yourself, you can't afford to be ill prepared. If you are more current in being in court, you can probably do that more easily than I have been able to do. I do think it is important to be in court some, but keep in mind that you are the district attorney, not a trial deputy, and that your first role is leadership. The people on the staff ought to be better than you at what they spend every day doing.

No human institutions are perfect, but some function better than others. The seven major elements of our criminal justice system are no exception. Like the good news-bad news stories, each has its strongest and weakest features. They include:

(1) **The Police**

The best aspect of the police is the basic dedication of the average officer to serve and protect. Their reasons for being cops do not include the pay, and cannot be explained as merely the power. They generally serve out of a commitment to a safe and responsible society.

The greatest improvement in the police function will come when lawmen come to understand that they are not an isolated, unappreciated minority, and should not so automatically close ranks to protect errant officers. When police officers will as readily report and testify against a fellow officer as any other citizen, true professionalism will have arrived.

(2) **The Defense**

As a group, defense lawyers have a zeal and ingenuity to protect their clients which is unmatched in any other country. That zeal and ingenuity are the defense lawyers' greatest strengths.

Their greatest weakness stems from those strengths: the pervasive view that almost any tactic or motion is acceptable if it might succeed, that justice is always subordinate to advocacy, and that each case is more black and white than grey. Changing those views will come more from the demands by the public than from within the legal profession.

(3) **The Prosecution**

The finest attribute of the prosecution is that it represents the ultimate reasonable person, society itself; the district attorney's duty, by law, is to achieve justice, not merely to convict. Given that luxury, it should be expected that prosecutors have a broader view of their role and of the search for the truth.

On the other hand, with the largely unchecked discretion given to prosecutors, the risk is ever-present of over-reaching and abuse of power. Abuses do occur, and it is incumbent upon the prosecutors to police their own with even more vigor than any other elements of our system. If they fail to do so diligently and daily, greater judicial control (and resulting red tape) will be thrust upon them.

(4) **The Judiciary**

Judges' strongest suit is also the strongest facet of jurors—their inherent desire to fashion a just result. That instinct for fairness is far more important than their grasp of the fine points of the law or the niceties of procedure.

Far and away the judiciary's greatest weakness is its momentum toward more procedures, hearings, reviews and mechanics. The judges are the only ones who can whittle down the the morass of details and delay. First, they must be committed to the adage that justice delayed is justice denied, and realize they are responsible for saying no to the increasing demands for form over substance.

(5) **Corrections**

Fortunately for all of us, corrections officials are optimists. They genuinely believe that most all offenders can be rehabiliated if they only had more resources with which to work. This spirit of optimism and hope represents the best aspect of our corrections industry.

The outstanding weakness of corrections is its blindness to an offender's crimes and the plight of past and future victims. Corrections officials simply must learn to distinguish good inmates from good risks for society. And they need to accept the fact that the state of the art has not yet reached the point that violent and career criminals can all be turned into productive citizens. Imprisonment remains a necessity.

(6) **The Media**

The strongest feature of our free press is its institutional standard that the free flow of information comes first, before the interests or reputation of any person or group. Because of that philosophy, which is ingrained from top to bottom in the media, we have little fear about the media being often subverted.

The glaring and growing weakness of journalism is the unwillingness or inability of management to control the excesses and bias of a generation of reporters who view their jobs as more investigative and interpretive than reportorial. More injustices and less public confidence will be the results if city editors and news directors don't do a better job of policing, correcting and disciplining their reporters.

(7) **The Public**

The public is not overawed with titles and our system. That healthy skepticism, and the public's broad view, are the bedrock strengths which will keep the lawyers, judges, corrections and police officers in check. It is the brightest asset of our overview.

The corresponding weakness is apathy. For a democracy to function, citizens must be willing to report crimes, be witnesses, serve on juries and be interested in supporting needed reforms. Leadership in the 80's and beyond has a tall order to fill in breaking down that apathy. But it can be done.

(8) **Overall**

Overall, our system deserves a B grade. When one considers how few countries and societies have ever achieved even this level, that's not a bad decade's work.

# VI

# A CANDID LOOK AT OUR JUDICIAL SYSTEM

In 1976, Dale spent a day in City Jail to better understand the system. He told reporters that "Boredom is the greatest problem." At lower left, Dale meets the press on the steps of the City and County Building.

# Chapter 14

# Judges and Juries, Grand and Otherwise

*Following 20 years of service as a member of the Supreme Court of Colorado I was employed by the legislature to recodify the Colorado Criminal Code. Soon after the work was completed I attended a Chinese New Year dinner where Dale Tooley introduced himself to me.*

*He said he had 50 deputy district attorneys on his staff who needed guidance in the enforcement of the new criminal code. He urged me to accept an appointment as his First Assistant.*

*I accepted the appointment as of March 1, 1973, and thereafter Dale Tooley and I worked very closely together on a daily basis. I knew him as well as any man. He was a man of action, a man of many talents, a great lawyer, a great public servant, a crusader for human rights and a man with the courage to advocate change.*

*The greatness of any man is measured by his kindness, by his education and intellect, by his modesty, by his dedication to duty and by the consideration and tolerance he has for others.*

*Measured by any or all of the scales I have mentioned, the life of Dale Tooley deserves high praise.*

— **Justice O. Otto Moore**

**Judges: An Unusual Breed**

Watching a good judge in action is like seeing a fine symphony conductor perform. The best judges are relatively passive in court and are able to move proceedings along with ease—and with occasional prodding of wordy counsel. The worst judges are those whose basic insecurity shows in the lengthy speeches made explaining each ruling, and who confuse impulsiveness for decisiveness.

One late Denver judge was known to say to a defendant about to be sentenced, "Stand up, Buster. I'm going to give you one that will rock you." By contrast, Judge Leonard Plank has a knack of handing down a stiff sentence in so nice a way that the defendant is appreciative.

Some judges take hours getting through their routine morning dockets. Others, like Judge Warren Martin, mastered the art of docket control quickly and set a record for the number of jury trials he could conduct in a year.

Next to newspaper reporters, judges have the thinnest skins of any participants in the system. In Colorado, the Bar Association's biennial poll of lawyers is designed to rate judges' performances, before the electorate votes on their fitness to be kept on the bench. Only rarely does the Bar poll have any effect whatever on the voters. Some say the best way for a judge to be retained is to have the opposition of the lawyers. Yet judges regularly lose sleep over such polls.

Judges also think the entire world reads and remembers the brief references in the press to appellate court reversals of their decisions. In fact, those are probably the least-read items in newspapers.

At a late night grand jury session, the judge and I were urging an attorney to end his delaying tactics and put his subpoenaed, immunized client on the witness stand. In an obvious effort to get more time, the lawyer stood up and announced loudly, "If we're going to get railroaded, I'm leaving!" As he reached the door, the judge pleaded, "Please, please, Don. Don't get mad." An hour later, over a beer, the lawyer and I laughed over the success of his theatrics.

Judges quickly become cloistered, in part because of their over-sensitivity to any appearance of impropriety. Many are nervous even having lunch with lawyers they have known for years.

Because of their relative isolation, judges are not the best instruments of social change. By training, judges become immersed in detail. A vivid example is the federal judge in an Eastern city who carefully weighed his decision on what type of tennis balls the school district should use. On the other hand, there are judges who think nothing should ever change and who generally agree with the philosophy that "change, at any time, at any place, for any reason should be deplored." An example of this inertia is the long time it took to persuade judges in Denver to permit the use of "Juror" badges. All too frequently, lawyers and witnesses in the courthouse would discuss a case within the hearing of a juror. No one knew who were jurors because they wore no badges. In 1974, we proposed use of such badges. It was not agreed to until 1981—and we had to raise private funds to pay for them.

What makes judges memorable is not their wisdom, their decisions or their errors. It is their idiosyncrasies. Judge Martin follows trial testimony closely while completing coloring books. During one long trial, the jury gave the judge a box of crayons after noticing how quickly he was using up his present stock.

A now-retired judge with a reputation for innovative short-cuts once said as our trial was about the begin, "Gentlemen, I'd like to handle this case without taking any testimony."

Judge James Flanigan enjoyed a well-deserved reputation for punctuality. He would appear on the bench at the stroke of 8:30 a.m. and sit in deadly silence until the last, uncomfortable lawyer arrived in court. His way of dealing with delaying tactics where lawyers claimed scheduling conflicts was to offer to hear matters at 7 a.m. or earlier. The scheduling conflicts resolved themselves quickly.

We had put together a strong case to close an establishment where every illegal act imaginable had occurred. The judge carefully read all the affidavits, then said, "Mr. Tooley, I'm going to order this terrible place closed. But I have one question. What is fellatio?" After the explanation, which seemed to fascinate him, he signed the order with the comment, "My word. What will they think of next?"

Judges from smaller communities enjoy coming to Denver. My experience is that they perform particularly well, in part to prove that rural judges didn't just fall off a turnip truck. Sometimes they prepare even too well. After a week-long trial to an out-of-town judge, we made extensive closing arguments. The judge listened attentively, then took from his pocket notes he had made the night before and read his decision.

More than most people, judges enjoy the out-of-the-ordinary, perhaps because they deal with so much routine. We conducted a complicated heroin ring investigation, involving both grand jury work and a court-authorized wiretap. A large shipment of heroin was believed to be en route from Mexico to Denver in an automobile which our investigators were tracking by air. To obtain necessary warrants and orders, we twice interrupted the same judge on the golf course on a Friday afternoon. Each time, he affably put down his clubs and dealt with the legal matters, once as detectives jogged alongside his golf cart.

Judges' sentencing practices usually become tougher as they see more victims and crime, particularly if the judge himself has become a victim. One defendant stole a judge's wallet from his chambers and another stole a judge's checkbook and forged and passed the checks. Inmates talk about how those acts may have contributed to their own longer sentences.

Another important factor in a judge's sentencing decision is the press. Judges will adamantly deny it, but experienced trial lawyers know that if a reporter is in the courtroom on sentencing day, the judge will be particularly careful not to let a lenient sentence slip by.

Denver has a very high level of education. It may be in part because of that quality that the system in general, and judges in particular, work better in Denver than most places. There may also be a tradition that the public expects judges to perform competently. Or it may be that citizens in Denver consider judges to be part of the government, which they are, and are not reluctant to criticize them loudly when they have it coming—and sometimes even when they don't.

## Juries and the Jury System

Juries are designed to be the conscience of the community. That they work as well as they do is more a tribute to the citizenry than to the system.

Almost without exception, jurors take their service seriously, do their best to achieve justice and try to follow the legalese of the judge's instructions. Even while I served as district attorney, my wife was selected to serve on a jury in a civil case. She refused to discuss the case with me in any respect while the trial was going on, because those were the judge's instructions. I didn't pursue it until the trial was over, for fear she would report me to the court. She was typical of the conscientiousness of jurors.

Skeptics say that a jury is as weak as the weakest juror. The opposite is more often true, because a jury's collective recollection of the evidence is as good as that of the best juror. The jury verdicts which defy logic are relatively rare, and are often the result of an honest misunderstanding of the complex legal instructions.

An example of a jury which rose above its weakest members is the coroner's jury which considered the death of Sidney Whitecrane, an American Indian. Whitecrane died following his arrest and altercation at the Gin Mill, a low-class bar in lower downtown Denver. I decided to use a coroner's inquest to determine the cause of death. A coroner's jury is a somewhat archaic procedure, but it is public, which grand jury proceedings are not. Suspicion had been raised about the role of the police and deputy sheriffs in Whitecrane's death, and the Indian community was anxious to have a public airing of the facts. The jury ruled that the cause of death was not felonious.

After the verdict, we asked the jury foreman to address our staff at one of our regular monthly training sessions. He explained that one of the jurors was almost deaf (a fact which the juror concealed from the lawyers) and that another had a decided anti-Indian bias reminiscent of the Old West. Even with those two uncharacteristically bad jurors, the jury's decision was a reasoned one consistent with the facts.

The best examination of prospective jurors will not always reveal their peculiarities. Mid-way through a long trial, the judge decided to sequester (lock up) the jury due to extensive publicity about certain inadmissible evidence. We had spent a full week picking the jury, and I was convinced there was nothing about any juror we hadn't asked. However, one of the jurors objected to the sequestration order unless he could figure out a way to feed daily his pet tarantula. An innovative bailiff made arrangements for the daily feedings so that the trial could proceed.

A defense lawyer once asked a prospective juror if she had any prejudice toward the lawyer's ethnic group. "Not until I met you," she replied brusquely.

Prosecutors get to know grand jurors well because the jurors' terms are for a full year and they meet weekly. For several months I watched a grand jury foreman administer the oath to scores of witnesses. He was one of our best foremen, but something seemed unusual about each oath he administered. When I learned his hobby was reading palms, I realized why he seemed to be examining so closely each witness' raised hand.

The relationship between lawyers and trial juries is a fragile one. Because half the lawyers appearing before a jury lose, lawyers can be some of the jury system's worst critics.

Many defense lawyers believe a juror cannot be fair and impartial if he has heard or read anything of the case. In fact, my experience is that jurors separate easily and clearly what they have heard or read about a case outside the courtroom from evidence and testimony in court. We began to have an abundance of defense motions for changes of venue due to pretrial publicity. We then adopted a general policy that we would agree to those venue changes. Suddenly, those motions were much fewer and farther between. In one bombing case, we consented to a venue change to Eastern Colorado. After one look at the prospective jurors there, the defense successfully pleaded with the judge to return the case to Denver for trial.

Lawyers revel in the jury selection process, during which they voir dire (French for "question") the prospective jurors. In theory, the purpose is to make certain that the jurors selected are fair and impartial. In practice, most lawyers use the opportunity to begin educating the jurors to their own theory of the case. In some cases, selecting the jury takes longer than presenting the evidence.

Jurors often complain about the duration and irrelevancy of such questioning. Those same jurors have called me after trials are over to find out if the trial deputy is single, if his eyes are really that blue, and even whether the pregnant woman trial deputy had a girl, a boy or twins.

What our system needs is not fewer jury trials, but more of them. The system can be improved by using plain, understandable English in legal instructions to the jury. Jurors should more often be permitted to take notes. It improves their attention and their recollection of the evidence, especially in a long trial. Jury views of crime scenes should more frequently be sought and granted. Many people have difficulty visualizing a location from word pictures alone.

Lawyers should make greater use of visual aids—charts,

graphs, slides and videotape. Nothing captures a jury's attention more than photographs admitted in evidence and circulated by the bailiff among the jurors.

The fees paid to jurors in Colorado are tragically low: three dollars a day while waiting and six dollars a day while sitting on a case. Our jurors' fees have been raised only twice since the 1890's. Despite repeated attempts, the legislature regularly manages to kill the juror fee increase bills while passing the legislators' own salary increase bills.

In the case of juries, we get far more than we pay for.

### The Grand Jury: Why It's Still Grand

The grand jury came into being in England to provide a bulwark against unfair charges by the King. Our Founding Fathers brought this institution to this country. Ironically, England has since abolished it, while it remains alive here. In the federal system and in some states, a defendant has a constitutional right, if he is to be charged with a felony offense, to have it brought by a grand jury. In Denver, and in a growing number of progressive jurisdictions, one percent or less of all felony cases are presented to the grand jury. In a high volume system, it is simply more practical to bring charges based on the district attorney's authority.

Most police departments and prosecutors have no subpoena power. Thus, a witness can (and not infrequently does) tell authorities to "buzz off," that he chooses not to talk. In some subcultures, talking with the law is considered treason. However, a grand jury does have the power of subpoena, and it is this fail-safe which often prevents important information from being permanently withheld.

We were investigating a complex kickback scheme involving an organized labor group and some private businesses. A key witness may also have been involved, so before we served him with a grand jury subpoena, I cleared it with his lawyer. No problem, the lawyer said, go ahead and serve him. We did so, and the next day he drove his car off a mountain highway west of Denver and was tragically killed in what was an apparent suicide. The prospect of being ordered to appear before a grand jury can be a frightening experience.

Where there are charges of abuse of the grand jury, they

most often involve federal prosecutors and federal grand juries. Elected prosecutors less often ask the grand jury to rubber stamp charges for filing. Also, many states have enacted grand jury reform laws—which the Justice Department has consistently opposed—such as permitting a witness to have his lawyer accompany him into the grand jury room, and requiring that all the proceedings be reported verbatim, with no off-the-record discussions between the jurors and the prosecutor.

Before these reforms in Colorado, the witness had to leave the grand jury room whenever he wanted to confer with his counsel. It was not uncommon for a witness to step out each time he was asked his name, address or occupation. The original theory of keeping the witness' lawyer out in the hallway was to preserve the secrecy of the proceedings. That goal never was accomplished. Under the old system, I have seen defense lawyers have their clients leave the room after each question, dictate into a recorder the question asked and the answer to be given, and then return to the courtroom. It has been far superior to have everyone in the same room, even though the witness' lawyer is allowed only to confer with his client, not argue or question witnesses.

Those who work with grand juries develop an abiding respect for the common sense and good judgment of the average citizen. One prospective grand juror told the judge she had only a sixth-grade education and couldn't possibly understand or deal with public corruption, securities fraud and other subjects the grand jury was to address. The judge nonetheless selected her. She proved to be one of the strongest jurors, whose questions to witnesses frequently covered points the prosecutor had missed. Wisdom and education are not synonymous.

Because a judge is not present while the grand jury is in session, the foreman presides and administers the oath to the witnesses. One year the judge selected a young public school teacher, a woman, as foreman. She served expertly, but throughout the year she was alternately referred to as "foreman," "forewoman," and "foreperson." One of the jurors tried to eliminate the confusion by addressing her as "madam forething."

Serving on a grand jury is a great learning experience. One afternoon a murderer testified in detail about his stabbing to death of a young mother as part of a contract murder. The shock was apparent on the jurors' faces. When their term was completed, they confided that seeing that side of life was something they would never have imagined.

Grand juries can play a unique role not only in investigations, but also in causing changes in government operations. One day a contractor named Raymond Franklin came to my office and said he was being solicited for a payoff in exchange for the questions and answers to a Denver Building Department license examination. He agreed to cooperate in the investigation and took marked money to the payoff exchange. The transaction occurred as promised, and that evening Art Stratton, a mayoral appointee, was being questioned before the grand jury. His conviction and those of almost a dozen others were a direct result of the testimony he gave that night. The grand jury then issued a series of reports, which were for the most part followed, on how to clean up that department. Unfortunately, Colorado grand juries have since that time been gagged. The legislature passed a law prohibiting grand jury reports after an Arapahoe County grand jury issued a report sharply critical of the county commissioners.

The Watergate era fundamentally changed the grand jury process. Suddenly the public, including prospective grand jurors, saw that a grand jury could make a difference, even if the subjects of the investigation included the President and the Attorney General. That new attitude of independence has been a healthy development.

One of our grand juries was conducting an investigation of illegal trafficking in babies. We asked for authority to issue a subpoena for some adoption records, and told the jury that, without that information, we could not put a case together. The grand jury deliberated on and denied our request, explaining that the confidentiality of adoption records was more important than this case. The decision may have been a correct one. It certainly would have been unheard of before the Watergate era, when juries had exercised little independence.

Only once in the history of the FBI has the agent-in-charge—along with many of his senior agents—been subpoenaed before a grand jury, advised of his right to remain silent and interrogated. That occurred in Denver after FBI informant Timothy Redfearn confessed to breaking into the Socialist Workers Party

(SWP) headquarters. Redfearn went to prison, but there was not enough evidence to prove the knowledge of the FBI agents in the break-ins. Therefore, the grand jury issued a tough, lengthy report which received appropriate attention from a U.S. Senate committee and from the FBI Director.

The independence of the grand jury showed in the foreman's questioning of one of the FBI agents, who had testified that he saw nothing wrong with a break-in committed by one of the SWP members, with whom the agent made the analogy of an invited guest.

"If I invited you to my home, and you took some of the silver, would that be theft?" asked the foreman.

"No," replied the agent. "That would be like borrowing it."

"Well," continued the foreman, "what if I instructed you that you were not to take the silver, and you still took it?"

"That still would not be theft," argued the agent. "It would be like borrowing—like taking an ash tray from a Las Vegas casino."

Predictably, the grand jury's report included a section on the need for better training of agents in the right and wrong of their informants' conduct.

Grand juries are grand when the district attorney doesn't try to control them.

### Technicalities

Nothing more enrages the public, police and prosecutors than technicalities. Taken to their illogical conclusions, they often result in dismissal of charges and release of the guilty.

No fair-minded person would argue that evidence should be admitted at any price, or that our fundamental commitment to fair play be diminished. What is needed is a better balance between seeking the truth, on the one hand, and doing so in a fair manner, on the other. As the following examples indicate, we are far too often out of balance.

Denver judges, like judges everywhere, spend more court time hearing motions and handling the procedural aspects of cases than they do in trial. One reason is the system's willingness to consider almost any hair-brained motion. One enterprising defense lawyer once persuaded a judge to hear his motion to dismiss a drunk driving charge on the ground that his client was too drunk to form the intent to drive while drinking. And it is not uncommon for defense lawyers to file motions to suppress evidence obtained through a search warrant, even where there was no search or warrant.

One reason for the excessive motions practice is that bizarre motions sometimes are granted, even in important cases. Such was the case in the contract murder prosecution of Michael Borrelli, a former New York City detective charged with the contract murder in Denver of his business partner, Hal Levine. The jury which convicted him of the murder included a woman who was less than candid during jury selection about whether she had ever in the past used drugs or had emotional problems. When this came to light after the trial, Borrelli's lawyer sought reversal of the conviction and a new trial. Other jurors reported that she was a rational juror, and no one suggested she had used drugs near the time of the trial nor while serving as a juror. Still, a new trial was granted. An acquittal in the second trial came as no surprise, because most cases prosecuted a second time after a delay of several years result in acquittals.

The exclusionary rule is a judge-made policy which says that if the magistrate or police officer blunders in obtaining evidence, even though the blunder may be slight and unintentional, the evidence may be kept from the jury. The result is that the defendant is rewarded and the public punished.

One of literally thousands of examples is a drug case where narcotics detectives watched a stream of people visit a suspected drug dealer's home on Quince Street. Two young people leaving the house admitted that they had just bought drugs there, that they had done so often, and that the seller (Clarence) had just said he received a new shipment. They gave the detectives a business card which the drug dealer had given them. It read, "Clarence, the Smoke Man," and it gave a telephone number. The substance bought by the two young people proved to be illegal drugs. The detectives included these facts in an affidavit and dutifully secured a search warrant from a judge. They seized a large quantity of illegal drugs, a drug scale, drug paraphernalia and a package of "Smoke Man" business cards. The drug-pushing case against Clarence was dismissed because the judge ruled that the evidence from the search was inadmissible under the exclusionary rule. The court said there was no proof before the search that Clarence had any of his new shipment left after the sale to the two young people. How such rulings could ever deter improper police conduct is a mystery.

As a result of a long line of such cases, we helped to draft and pass a state law which modifies the harshness of the exclusionary rule. It says simply that evidence obtained through police conduct "taken in a reasonable, good faith belief that it was proper" should not be thrown out of court. It is a reasonable and necessary step toward returning balance to our system.

The public usually believes that judges are responsible for all the technicalities. In fact, legislatures share that responsibility. Not every wrong is or should be a crime. Indeed, I testified many times against creating new crimes which would be low priority and would clog our system. Once, the legislature almost made it a criminal offense to smoke in a public building. On another occasion a legislator proposed that any sexual intercourse within 500 feet of a school be made a crime—even though many people live within 500 feet of a school.

However, some important statutory loopholes have prevented prosecutions.

One summer afternoon two juvenile offenders ran from their guards as they were entering Juvenile Hall. They were captured when they forgot that they were handcuffed to one another and ran on opposite sides of a utility pole. The loophole was that it was no offense to escape from a juvenile facility. The only charge then fileable was attempted theft of the handcuffs—a charge we declined to file.

When loopholes are closed, it helps only as to future cases. For example, the Colorado Supreme Court ruled that confidential medical records, stolen and sold to insurance companies for more than $2 million each year, did not constitute a "thing of value" under the Colorado criminal laws. The closing of the loophole by the legislature did not reinstate the criminal cases against the insurance companies.

In this country, one cannot commit a crime by sheer accident. There must be an act, coupled with a criminal mental state. A prominent Pennsylvania businessman was caught in a Denver motel room in the final stages of a transaction with a prostitute. Thinking he was still in the East, he attempted to bribe the police officers who arrested him. He then found himself charged with bribery, as well. With as straight a face as possible, his lawyer argued that his client, while sober enough to carry on with the hooker, was not sober enough to have formed the intent to bribe the police officers. Before the trial ended, he pleaded guilty. His innovative view of criminal intent did earn him probation rather than a prison sentence.

Juries also make some peculiar decisions about criminal intent. Several years ago, two young women robbed an elderly Denver businessman in his apartment on the top floor of the Navarre. When he attempted to stop them only a minute or two after the robbery, one of the women bludgeoned him to death. She plead not guilty by reason of insanity to the charges of robbery and murder. The jury concluded that she was sane when she committed the robbery, but insane a minute or two later when she beat the old man to death. As a result, she was sent to the State Hospital in Pueblo rather than to a penal facility. Those jurors were part of the same public which complains about technicalities.

What is often viewed as a technicality is often simply a lack of evidence. Our judicial system deals with what is provable, the public with what is probable.

Occasionally more proof of a crime can be developed before trial, but usually not. We once prepared a case to close the Outlaw Bar in lower downtown. The first complaints were that the hookers operating out of the bar were so active that they were stopping traffic during rush hours. A fire bombing then occurred, and there were other violent acts. One Saturday morning as we reviewed the case, I said, "This isn't strong enough. What we really need is evidence of drug dealing on the premises." With that we adjourned to the Outlaw Bar, surprisingly received permission to search, and uncovered a supply of "white crosses" and other illegal drugs. The court then ordered the bar closed the following Monday.

An establishment almost as bad as the Outlaw Bar was Satan's on Market Street. It operated a "champagne bust-out scheme." Customers paid $50 for a bottle of champagne and received the promise (and often the fact) of sexual favors in return. The staff said our case against the establishment was weak because the citizens/victims were unwilling to testify. "Nonsense," I said. "Give me the file and I'll call the witnesses and try the case." Although we tried and won the case, I could not bring myself to call those witnesses who said that, if they testified about their extra-curricular activities at Satan's, they would lose their marriages, jobs, and in one case, the opportunity to see the grandchildren.

It is true that sometimes police and prosecutors blame technicalities for absence of evidence. But it is equally true that our system has moved too much toward form over substance. To the greatest degree possible, ours should be a search for the truth rather than a trial of the investigation. Because of our office's remarkable Appellate Division headed by persuasive Brooke Wunnicke and former Chief Justice O. Otto Moore, our appellate success rate was 90%. As much as anything, that record helped to maintain a degree of sanity in Colorado's system of criminal justice.

# Chapter 15

# Other Actors in the System: The Police, The Media and the Innocent

## The Police

Anyone who works closely with a large police department for a number of years comes to admire the basic dedication of the typical police officer. One also learns that police officers are fascinated with weaponry, radio communications (in order to be in instant communication with the entire department), automobiles (the faster the better), unique investigative tools (such as wiretaps, body bugs and grand jury subpoenas), and most of all, officers are fascinated with action on the street. Most officers are far more dedicated to the "action" of the war against crime than to the drudgery of meticulous gathering of evidence.

Over ten years, we never lacked for officers to participate in a raid, execute a search warrant or close an establishment. Whenever there is action, officers come out of the woodwork. At 2 a.m. one St. Patrick's Day, violence erupted around the Capitol Hill headquarters of the militant Crusade for Justice. One officer was critically wounded and a young Chicano killed following a routine traffic stop. A massive bomb explosion then ripped open apartments on Downing Street and gunfire continued for several hours, even as a large crowd gathered less than a block from the scene of the violence. I was impressed with how quickly and in what numbers officers arrived at the scene. When we concurred in an "exigent circumstances" search of the apartment complex, a parade of officers lined up to participate. Police officers regard courage as one of their highest values.

The flip side of courage is zeal, and the need to control it. Early on, we advised the Vice and Drug Control Unit that we would not prosecute vice or prostitution cases developed by an undercover detective becoming nude with the suspect or engaging in intimate relations with her. That policy, while followed, caused regular grumblings about our "handcuffing" the police and preventing use of the most effective—and undoubtedly the most interesting—techniques. However, never did a detective grumble about this policy when it came to investigating homosexual pimping activities.

More than once as part of a drug investigation, command officers sought permission to provide suspected drug manufacturers with raw materials for the manufacture of illegal drugs. We permitted it only if the suspects were kept under constant surveillance and they were arrested and the illicit drugs seized before reaching the streets. Faced with this restriction, some enterprising undercover detectives persuaded drug pushers to demonstrate to them the entire manufacturing process, which was captured on videotape by a concealed police camera.

Because of our system of checks and balances, there are limits which prevent the ends from justifying the means. An officer once came to my home to "clear with me" the fact that one of his bombing investigation informants would be throwing a bomb through the window of an innocent person's business establishment. The purpose was to keep some suspects satisfied that the undercover police informant was both bold and not a "snitch." The police plan was that the Bomb Squad would promptly remove the bomb and no further damage would result. We vetoed the plan, explaining that not even the authorities can enforce the law by breaking it. "That is what Watergate was all about," I said. We accomplished the goal without breaking the law or damaging property, and the investigation was a success.

The more specialized the law enforcement unit, the greater the officers' zeal. We particularly had difficulty with State Division of Wildlife officers. Two events caused me to issue an order requiring that no game and fish violations be filed without advance approval by our office. After court one day, a young deputy district attorney was toiling in our law library. He explained that he was in trial and was researching a unique problem in his misdemeanor case against a defendant charged with harassing a rabbit. He was trying to determine if he had to prove that this particular rabbit felt harassed, or only that any reasonable rabbit would have felt harassed. "How the hell did that case get into the office?" I asked. "Filed direct by the Wildlife officer," he replied.

Only a few months later, Wildlife officers filed almost 20

cases against parents who accompanied their children to the annual Huckleberry Finn Day in Washington Park. The children dressed up as Huckleberry Finn, Tom Sawyer or Becky Thatcher. An irrigation ditch in the park was stocked with trout, and prizes were given for the best costumes and for the biggest and most fish caught. Many of the children were too young to maneuver their fishing lines into the water, and were helped by their parents. Those parents were then charged with the crime of fishing without a license. The charges may have been quite provable, but they were grossly unjust. We dismissed all of those cases and put the Wildlife officers on a short leash. For some time, that department refused to stock adequately lakes in the Denver parks because of our "soft on crime" attitude toward fish and game law violators.

The problem was even more acute in outlying areas of the state. One district attorney in Southern Colorado received sharp criticism from Wildlife officers over a plea bargain. A hunter, out of season and without a license, shot two elk. When a Wildlife officer confronted the hunter at the scene, the hunter shot and wounded the officer. The district attorney required that the hunter plead guilty to first degree assault on the officer, and to the illegal killing of one of the elk. The charge involving the other elk was dropped. Wildlife officers vigorously complained that one of the most important charges had been dropped arbitrarily.

Zeal for action extends to white collar crime investigators, as well. We conducted a lengthy investigation to end usury practices of Denver pawnshops. For decades, they charged their customers interest at annual rates exceeding 120 per cent, in clear violation of state usury laws. In order to prove the charges, it was necessary to analyze literally thousands of pawn tickets and transactions. Keeping detectives on that task required heroic efforts on our part. But, at the same time, we were running a court-approved wiretap on the phone of a career criminal who was engaged in the wholesale fencing of stolen property. By contrast, every detective privy to the existence of the wiretap volunteered off-duty time to help out.

Police officers are also fascinated with informants, because they recognize them as essential to combatting crime. The difficulty is that the worse the crime, the worse the informant who knows something about it. Good citizens simply don't come in contact with contract murder and organized crime conspiracies. The most productive informants are often those trying to work off their own case. At times, I felt that if we could lock up all the informants, we might have the answer to crime.

Officers often develop close relationships with their informants. One night I joined officers in locating an informant-turned-safecracker, because we wanted to question him without delay. We located him at a West Denver nightspot, and the principal officer went inside to make the arrest. We waited two hours in the parking lot before the officer and the informant emerged when the establishment closed at 2 a.m. I asked what caused the delay. "I just hated to tell him he was under arrest," explained the officer.

Another problem with informants is that they are often working with competing law enforcement agencies. A case in point involved Timothy Redfearn, the career informant/burglar. For years, he was paid by the FBI as an informant.

Redfearn was an informant to other officers, as well—a fact which was underscored by the number of calls we received on his behalf after he was arrested. In fact, Redfearn wrote from the penitentiary asking for a job in the District Attorney's Office, because he had "learned so much about law enforcement" during his career.

There will always be risks with overzealousness, informant abuse and simple love of street action by police officers. Those risks pale in comparison to the crime problem our society would face if our police agencies were composed of placid, bored bureaucrats.

### Dealing With The Media: A Daily Event

The easiest part of dealing with reporters is laying down rules on how it should be done: Tell the truth, or say "no comment." Don't initiate calls to the media. Use press releases sparingly and news conferences almost never. Don't gag the staff and don't hire a press secretary. And unless already known, don't disclose the identity of subjects of an investigation. To these should be added: Be careful about jesting with the press.

One St. Patrick's Day a dispute arose over whether some enthusiastic parade participants could paint a green stripe down the center of the parade route. A radio reporter called and asked what I thought about it.

"Patrick, me lad," I responded, "this being St. Patty's Day, people can paint anything they want as green as they want, and there will be no prosecutions."

"Great," said the reporter. "I'll use that on the noon news."

"I was only kidding," I protested, to no avail. It was carried on the noon news as a special dispensation from the district attorney.

On another occasion, a newspaper reporter called (as they did daily) to see what was going on.

"We've filed a burglary case against Bishop Casey," I told her. The conversation moved on, and I failed to explain that "Bishop" was the first name of the burglary defendant, not the title of the respected leader of the Catholic Church in Colorado. Fortunately, the reporter called back to get more details, and I was able to prevent the publishing of a libelous story created through my misdirected jest.

The media is the public's representative, and is entitled to know what can properly be disclosed about the public's business. For that reason, an elected official must keep an eye on the role of the media. A good example involved a grand jury which was probing some alleged misspending of public funds. A former governor of the state became a focus of the investigation. We suggested that he appear a half hour before the grand jury convened, in order to avoid the press. He did so, and walked past an eager, but newly hired, reporter who did not recognize him. The former governor was not charged, and to this day the public does not know he was investigated.

The day before President Carter was to visit Denver, I received a letter from a man threatening to kill the President. We called the Secret Service. They were excited to have a threat to work on, because there had been little action. The writer proved to be a murderer, but we confirmed that he was safely locked up at the state penitentiary, with no early prospects of release. When the press learned of the event some weeks later, after it was no longer newsworthy, at least one reporter expressed unhappiness about not being "tipped off."

Early in my first term, my wife and I returned one day early from an out-of-town meeting. It was night when we arrived in Denver, so rather than disturb our babysitter, we checked into a Denver hotel. As we were checking in, a man was being captured and held in the lobby for having just robbed the place at gunpoint. Droves of police officers arrived, many of whom I knew. I took great pains to introduce my wife to each, and even to the armed robber, to dispel any rumors to the press that I was sleeping with a strange woman at a downtown hotel. In private life, that would not have been necessary.

A reporter once asked how we were coming on an investigation which the state had publicly turned over to us. I said that I had just that morning received the investigative report. The reporter knew investigative reports are not released, but still he asked if he could read it. I said, "Of course not." He then asked if I would simply leave it on my desk that night. When I said "Hell, no!", he replied that he "just felt a professional obligation to ask." That, however, was a rare occurrence.

A more typical technique is the reporter who calls, after having written an expose, and asks if we intend to investigate it. If we answer "no," the headline will read "DA Refuses to Investigate." If we answer "yes," the headline will say "DA to Probe Newspaper's Allegations." Neither would be accurate, because the office must first make a preliminary determination that the matter is potentially criminal, within the statute of limitations and occurred within the City and County of Denver. One of my chief deputies, Richard Spriggs, handled those calls best.

When asked for comment, he would say, "We read your story with interest." When asked for a more expansive statement, he would say, "We read your story with *great* interest."

Investigative reporters, perhaps naturally, lose their objectivity as they determine the thrust of their story. If there is petty wrongdoing, they believe, out of sincere zeal, that it should be treated as the crime of the century. And they are unhappy about the delays which occur with every professionally run criminal investigation.

A Denver newspaper reported that millions of dollars were being stolen from the Denver airport parking receipts. We had sent a surveillance team to the airport and did not develop evidence sufficient to support a criminal prosecution, although the procedures were sloppy and the city was obviously permitting money to slip through the cracks. The grand jury decided that the first step should be an audit, and since the city had already contracted for an expensive audit, both we and the grand jury felt further investigation should await that report. That decision was greeted with deep hostility by the reporter and his newspaper, a reaction which would not have been the case had it not been "their" scandal.

During the last several years, reporters seem to have become somewhat less innovative in gathering the news. In the early 70's, we commonly took devious routes to the location where a search warrant was to be executed because, more than occasionally, reporters would follow us from our offices. Once, a woman reporter asked to be allowed to observe a raid on an establishment we would be closing. Since she didn't report crime news, and because it was past her paper's deadline, I told her where we would be in one hour. She dutifully showed up ahead of time, was mistaken for a hooker, and was thrown out of the establishment.

The press has tremendous influence over the system, and the system operates better in the glare of publicity than in the secrecy of closed rooms. Thomas Jefferson was correct when he observed that he would prefer the press without the government than the government without the press, were those his choices.

That having been said, the media does not always act responsibly. The investigation of a mishandled pet cemetery (where the cemetery was burying dogs, cats and horses in the same pit) drew far more press and television attention than a number of murder verdicts, which went unreported. The unevenness in the proportions of a story are often dictated by which newspaper or station reported the story first.

The press' power, well used, is best illustrated by Fred Gillies, a reporter with The Denver Post. He took a bulldog approach to reporting mishandling of child abuse reports. More than any person in the state, he is responsible for a much-improved fabric of dealing with child abuse, from the Department of Social Services through the courts.

Dealing with the media can be trying, but it is a daily, and necessary, event.

**The "Innocent"**

The old-time radio program "Mr. District Attorney" began with a speech on the district attorney's duty to as vigorously protect the rights of the innocent as to prosecute the guilty. That is a duty which is taken seriously by the vast majority of prosecutors I know. Our standing policy was to reject or dismiss any case unless the evidence was sufficient to support a conviction. In addition, and equally important, the case was to be dropped if the deputy district attorney handling it believed the defendant was innocent. As a chief deputy once said at a staff meeting, "The public can't pay me enough to prosecute an innocent person."

In prosecuting 200,000 cases over a decade, it was not rare for the evidence to be (or become) too weak to support a prosecution. But it was exceedingly rare for a case to be filed against a truly innocent person. When that rare event would occur and be discovered, it sent shudders through the staff.

The police once arrested the director of Clayton College, a home for orphan boys, for investigation of sexual assault on a child. Something seemed strange about the case when one of the filing deputy district attorneys reviewed it. After screening hundreds of cases, these prosecutors became experts at spotting a questionable investigation. The file was sent up to me and I agreed that more investigation was needed. Even that did not satisfy us, so we called in the alleged victim, a teenage boy. On further questioning, it developed that he was angry at the director for not having adopted him. As he recounted the alleged assault, he told a story which scientifically could not possibly have occurred.

Because the director had been prematurely arrested by the police, the media had prominently carried stories about the case and the supposed assault. It seemed only fair that our decision that the director was innocent be given the same coverage. We called a rare news conference for that purpose. Unfortunately, it is like getting toothpaste back into the tube. No one knows if the prejudice and damage of a false accusation can ever be fully corrected by the truth.

The case against an innocent person which most stands out in my mind was a murder case. The body of a young woman was discovered under a car by school children in the Capitol Hill area of Denver. The investigating detective was convinced that the murderer was a man on whom the suspicion first focused. He directed his entire investigation to that end, and developed evidence strong enough to convict his suspect of murder.

One of our trial investigators and the deputy assigned to the case began their own investigation, despite bitter criticism from the homicide investigator, who was defensive about "his" investigation and case. The end result was an admission from the key witness that the defendant was in no way involved in the killing. We also uncovered other evidence corroborating the innocence of the defendant, whom we almost sent to prison for life.

On the other side of the innocence coin, defendants rationalize their criminal conduct as justified, and therefore the same thing as innocence.

A professional hockey player from Utah became involved in a violent fight on the ice during a game against the Denver Rockies. The entire game was a mass conflict, prompting one wag to describe it as a fight, at which a hockey game broke out. In frustration, the player hurled his hockey stick deep into the crowd, slicing a deep cut on the nose of a young child.

Contestants may be fair game for retaliation, but not kindergarten spectators. We charged the offending player with third degree assault. He was outraged at our decision and he and his lawyer demanded a meeting with me to discuss this unfairness. He left with an explanation, but not one bit convinced. To this day, he carries a criminal assault conviction on his record—one which we believe he richly deserved, but which he believes was a gross miscarriage of justice.

A Denver society leader allegedly contracted with a man to kill her husband. To this day I feel certain she planned and contracted for the murder. However, the tape recording of an incriminating conversation proved to have been altered. Given that development and the weakness of the remaining evidence, we dismissed the case. The husband and his family are convinced of her guilt and are angry at me for the dismissal of the case. The wife claimed innocence, and remains angry because the case was filed in the first place. The judge was angry because the case used up limited courtroom time in the pretrial stages. In some cases, you just can't win.

Under occasional unreasonable laws, some acts are criminal when they should not be. For example, legislators, unable to decide how to handle the offense of adultery, made it against the law, but then eliminated all penalties for it.

Some young people are particularly offended by laws against private possession and use of marijuana, which many of them consider to be innocent acts. It is true that if we locked up all people who have ever used marijuana, most of the generation under thirty would have jailhouse records.

We drafted an ordinance in 1974 to make private possession of a small amount of marijuana a simple city ordinance violation, similar to a traffic ticket, rather than a crime. The Denver City Council passed that pioneering law by a vote of 10 to 0.

The Council's action was even more remarkable because of the setting in which the vote occurred. We had drafted an ordinance to ban dealer sale of Saturday Night Special handguns. I made the mistake of scheduling both ordinances for debate and vote at the same City Council meeting. The handgun ordinance drew a large crowd of conservative opponents, many active in the National Rifle Association, who considered the proposal an infringement on their right to bear arms. The marijuana ordinance drew a large crowd of liberal supporters, many of whom were street people in long hair and sandals. The meeting was tense, and most of our witnesses fled in fear before testifying. One conservative shouted, "What's happened to you, Tooley? You want to legalize pot and take away our guns." In one of its finer moments, the Council passed both measures. Half the crowd left believing that innocent acts were now crimes, and the other half believing the opposite.

In our system, the presumption of innocence is more than words. It is an underlying philosophy which keeps most prosecutors from filing cases which may technically be crimes, but which in practice are innocent acts—or at least low priority offenses. Innocent citizens are protected daily by a system in which decisions are not computer-made, but rather are man-made. Civil libertarians should fight to keep it that way.

# Chapter 16

# Extraordinary People Who Make The System Work

## It's Better to Wear Out Than to Rust Out

In a lifetime, one comes to know only a very few people whose lives are dedicated to service, reform and justice. The most remarkable of this extraordinary breed is Judge O. Otto Moore. Born in the late 1800's, a descendant of Sir Walter Scott, he dedicated his life to the law and the fight against crime and injustice.

I first came to know Judge Moore when he was Chief Justice of the Colorado Supreme Court, where he was one of its most productive members for 20 years. Equally impressive was his leadership in 1972 in helping to pass a long-overdue state constitutional amendment which abolished justices of the peace and reorganized the state's judicial system.

When I was first elected district attorney in 1972, Judge Moore was my first choice as First Assistant. After retiring from the Supreme Court, he had written the new Code of Criminal Procedure and the Colorado Criminal Code. We persuaded him that he was needed. He accepted the appointment, saying, "Well, I think I could be of help to the young deputy district attorneys. And I'd rather wear out than rust out."

His spirit of youth and adventure is nourished by his wife, Cherie, whom he married while he was a soldier in World War I. The union is a success story, although it began with Judge Moore in the brig for going AWOL to marry her. She is a pioneer in her own right. She smoked and was an executive at the University of Denver long before either was acceptable conduct for a woman. It is she, as much as her husband, who has maintained their yearly travel tradition. Not many couples in their 80's look forward to riding camels in Egypt.

He continues to play tennis regularly. At age 85, I recall his muttering to himself, after hitting a ball into the net, "I've got to work on my backhand."

Humor has helped keep him young. Once, while writing the Criminal Code, he was asked at a legislative hearing to explain the difference between fornication and adultery. The national press carried his jestful, spontaneous response: "I don't know. I do know a fellow who tried both and couldn't tell the difference."

After returning from World War I, Judge Moore joined the staff of then Denver district attorney, Philip S. Van Cise. Van Cise and Moore began a crusade against the Ku Klux Klan, which had seized control of the Republican Party and of many public offices. Judge Moore remembers in detail a sad chapter in Denver history when, in a single day, more than 5,000 citizens were inducted into the Klan at a field which is now Overland Golf Course. Only after persistent efforts were we able to persuade him to make a video tape of his recollections of his successful fight against the Klan. It is now a part of the Western History Collection of the Denver Public Library.

His experience with the Prohibition era served the District Attorney's Office well as we struggled with the best way to handle marijuana cases which, like Prohibition cases, were the product of widespread disobedience of a law. "Marijuana is like whiskey in the Prohibition era," he said at a Chief Deputies' staff meeting, "Possession, possession for sale, and sale. Possession should not be much of a crime." That influence was a force to amend both Denver and Colorado law to end sentences of imprisonment for simple possession of small amounts of marijuana.

One day, the discussion of marijuana and prohibition cases reminded him that, as a young deputy district attorney, he had often smashed contraband whiskey in the basement of the District Attorney's Building. "I'll bet we could still smell it down there," he said. We went downstairs and raised many eyebrows as we sniffed in vain for the scent of days gone by.

He simply doesn't hold grudges. "Life is too short," he says. One night at a North Denver restaurant I watched him greet and hug an elderly Italian gentleman. "Chubby, it's been a long time. You look good," exclaimed Judge Moore.

"I've followed your career. You've done great," the man responded.

The two men had not seen one another for almost 50 years, since Judge Moore had prosecuted Chubby and sent him to prison in the 30's.

Judge Moore serves as a living example of integrity, without piety. He describes his days as operator of Denver streetcars as he worked his way through college, saying, "We charged five cents per passenger, some of which we turned in to the company." In truth, he never took so much as a penny which did not belong to him.

An example of his integrity was his resignation as a deputy district attorney in the depth of the Great Depression. He had prosecuted some whiskey manufacturers, and the landlady of the house where the whiskey was made was joined as a technical defendant. The then-district attorney had assured Moore that the case against the landlady would be dismissed if the jury should surprisingly find her guilty. The jury found all of the defendants guilty, including the old lady. When the district attorney reneged on his promise to dismiss the case against her, Moore immediately wrote out his resignation and walked out of the District Attorney's Office and into the Depression without a job and with less than ten dollars to his name. After setting up a law practice, he carried to the Supreme Court the cause to free the landlady from her penitentiary sentence, without success. Her imprisonment was a miscarriage of justice which still troubles him deeply more than half a century later.

One night after he had left the District Attorney's Office, while walking home from work, he struck up a conversation with an elderly man. The old man described vividly fears common to older people: fear of the poor farm and fear of financial insecurity in their twilight years. This was before the era of Social Security. Moore did what few people do about their social concerns. He acted on them.

In a few short years, without any compensation and with little thanks, he organized a grassroots drive which brought Colorado a pension system by constitutional amendment. At least twice, a powerful coalition of corporate and business interests attempted to repeal the Colorado pension. Each time Moore organized thousands of citizens throughout the state to fight the special interests. Each time he succeeded, saving the earliest model of a sound state pension program for senior citizens. In the course of these battles, he was vilified in the press. He responded by publishing hundreds of thousands of copies of a weekly seniors publication of his own. His account of this crusade can be found in his book, Mile High Harbor.

Even though age is a state of mind and not a time of life, I was conscious of the fact that Judge Moore was in his 80's, and that most people lose some mental sharpness at that age. I decided to sit in on an oral argument which he was scheduled to make in an important case before the Colorado Supreme Court.

Appellate judges often take pleasure in interrupting counsel's arguments to pose questions. As he began his argument, Judge Moore was interrupted by a question from the Chief Justice. "I will come to that issue in just a moment," roared Judge Moore.

"I'm sorry, Judge," responded the Chief Justice. It was a complete reversal of the ordinary exchange between court and counsel. Judge Moore made an excellent presentation. We won the case. There was no doubt about his alertness and ability as an advocate.

### A Casualty of the War Against Crime

Kenneth Patrick Brown is a casualty of the war against crime. For two decades, his genius made him one of the most productive undercover agents in the history of the state. As any undercover officer will tell you, the pressure and stress of leading two lives are enormous. The breaking point always comes well before retirement. Brown's came after two decades of remarkable service.

It was in 1973 that I first met Brown as he walked into a meeting of the Colorado Bureau of Investigation. He had just broken a massive drug ring after months of dangerous undercover work. He was walking with a cane because of his enormous weight—300 pounds on his five foot, seven inch frame. In the following years, I saw his weight fluctuate from 130 to 300 pounds and back again. He used the alteration of his appearance to advantage.

For several weeks he worked undercover in the state penitentiary, posing as an inmate. His mission was to break up a crime ring operating within the walls. An inmate he had arrested and sent to prison several years earlier confronted Brown.

"Don't I know you from somewhere?" the inmate asked.

"Never seen you before, buddy," Brown responded. The

inmate accepted the denial because the agent who arrested him had weighed twice as much.

When he was at peak weight, before joining the CBI, he was able to conceal a gun in his buttocks. Two criminals who had discovered his true identity took him to a remote area and were threatening to kill him. He shot them with the gun he had concealed in his own fat.

In the late 60's and early 70's, dozens of fires destroyed millions of dollars' worth of buildings under construction in the Denver area. These came to be known as the condominium fires. Almost all of them occurred at nonunion construction projects. The Denver grand jury and also federal agencies worked endlessly on the investigation, but without success. That the fires were a result of labor racketeering was commonly assumed, but no labor official would talk.

A labor organizer named Anthony Mulligan was sent to Denver from the international headquarters of a building trades union. He became the object of suspicion when he would regularly come to work in a red suit the day following a condominium fire. In addition, the fires often occurred shortly after a labor organizer had called on the nonunion contractor and had been told that the contractor was not interested in making the project a union job.

Because none of the usual investigative techniques had worked, arrangements were made to assign Brown to the case in a last-ditch effort to solve it. He assumed the role of a reputed organized crime figure from Detroit, complete with a Michigan identity, license plates and all the trappings. The trappings included money for a flamboyant life style. Brown was good, but his investigations were not cheap to run.

During much of the investigation he wore a body microphone which transmitted to agents in a vehicle some distance away. As Brown's fellow agents listened, the conversations were recorded. (This is a lawful procedure without a court order in Colorado and in most states, so long as one of the principal participants to the conversation consents. Of course, the consenting participant was Brown, not Mulligan.)

Brown located Mulligan at a North Denver bar and struck up a conversation with him. Quickly, they compared weapons and soon had become fast friends. Brown accompanied Mulligan to a union convention in Canada. The script called for Brown to avoid any discussion of the condominium fires until Mulligan broached the subject. Brown carefully followed the script.

The next part of the elaborate plan was an appearance by Carl Whiteside, Deputy Director of the CBI, along with a fellow agent. They came to Brown's hotel room posing as underlings while Mulligan was there. They delivered to Brown a suitcase full of bills to pay him for a completed "job." Brown asked Mulligan to help him count the cash, which in reality was the CBI's entire "flash roll." When Mulligan announced the total of less than $100,000, Brown raged over being swindled.

"I ought to blow up their operation!" Brown shouted.

"Blow it up? Why not burn it down?" Mulligan offered.

This began a long series of discussions and admissions by Mulligan, all on tape. At one point Mulligan drove Brown to some of the fire sites. In the end, those tapes constituted the key evidence which convicted Mulligan and which led to convictions of several of his confederates.

As often happens, the investigation expanded as Brown was introduced to Edward Urioste, a labor official with the New Mexico building trades. Urioste supplied dynamite to be used in the planned destruction of a Denver shopping center. What Urioste didn't know was that Brown was a CBI agent and the plane in which they flew the dynamite through a storm to Denver was a state-owned plane. At the appropriate time, when Urioste was within the City and County of Denver, Brown shocked Urioste, saying, "I'm the man. You're history. I'm putting you in chains"—cop talk for saying that Brown was a lawman and had the evidence on Urioste, who was about to be handcuffed. Mulligan, Urioste and the others convicted were sentenced to the penitentiary, but served only short terms.

Brown continued to roll up successes. He was increasingly temperamental and expensive, but he was too good to bench. He began to use more variations of his Mafia member role. He was instrumental in breaking up the Texas Mafia in Denver.

My first hard evidence that Brown was becoming a crime war casualty came during a cab ride from Salt Lake City Airport to a downtown hotel. Brown was heading a group of undercover investigators working out of our office who were probing nursing home and Medicaid fraud. We flew to Salt Lake City one Saturday to confront, serve indictment papers on and question a prominent pharmacist who was engaged in Medicaid fraud in Denver.

The cab driver mentioned in passing that he was a rugby player. Brown, at that time weighing less than 150 pounds, immediately assumed the role of a professional rugby player. For the full fifteen minute ride he carried on the pretense. I was convinced he was not trying to impress us; rather, he was losing the focus of his own true identity.

Only a few months later, the years of pressure became even more apparent. Brown was again posing as a member of organized crime. He was sharing a downtown hotel room with a major land swindler suspect. It was clear from the tapes that Brown was drinking to excess and was not following the script. We arranged a meeting at a quiet place on East Sixth Avenue to discuss the investigation. Brown showed up late, and drunk, and in the presence of a cab driver he openly identified himself and discussed the investigation. I promptly terminated the investigation, and our use of Brown.

Not long after that, Brown left the CBI for medical reasons. He took a law enforcement position in a town in Wyoming. One night in a bar, he pulled his gun and loudly announced that he was Kenny Brown, a lawman. Alternately, he shouted he was an Italian from Detroit. The true Kenneth Patrick Brown was lost in the pressure of endless and dangerous undercover work in the war against crime. Had this occurred on the battlefield, Brown would have received both a Purple Heart and the Congressional Medal of Honor.

# Chapter 17

# Prisons and Punishment

## Prisons

Since civilization began, we have searched for the best ways to deal with those who violate society's rules. We seem torn between punishment and rehabilitation, although they are not necessarily inconsistent. Both seek the same end result of deterring crime.

The difficulty is that we don't yet know how to rehabilitate the most serious offenders. Until we learn how, a free society requires that violent and career criminals be isolated from the rest of us.

In America, we give weak support to prison industries and inmate work programs which have been conducted for decades in other countries. In the Soviet Union, our delegation of U.S. prosecutors saw prisoners hard at work constructing furniture in a Leningrad prison. In Shanghai, we watched thousands of prisoners turn out watches and clothing. The profits from the sale of those products reportedly paid all the operating costs of the prison. In both countries, their recidivism rate is apparently far less than our own.

In this country, corrections officers regard a prisoner's conduct in prison as the best measure of how he will do when released; but, the best prisoners are often the worst citizens. Harry Hoptoff was a six-time loser. As a career burglar, we identified him for priority attention under our Career Criminal program. (Some Department of Corrections officials referred to Hoptoff and others like him as "career consumers of correctional services.") A prison diagnostic report accurately said of Hoptoff: "Harry is an excellent inmate. But he is a lousy citizen."

For years—and perhaps it still goes on—inmates at the Denver County Jail smuggled to their cells generous helpings of bread, sugar and jelly from the dining hall. These raw materials were then placed in water in plastic containers. The fermented product kept many prisoners in a mild state of intoxication.

At the state penitentiary at Canon City, a ring of inmates conducted a large heroin sales business from behind the walls. An investigation revealed that heroin was regularly smuggled into the prison by submerging plastic baggies of heroin in canisters of milk. State health regulations, which prohibited opening of the canisters, created a free passage for the contraband drugs.

Sometimes prisoners talk their way out of prison. Before Colorado essentially abolished parole as an early release mechanism, articulate inmates often persuaded the Parole Board to release them far earlier than expected. In one neighboring state, while the Parole Board was chaired by a recovered alcoholic, no inmate was paroled unless he was involved in Alcoholics Anonymous—whether or not the inmate drank.

A travel agent from India swindled scores of travel customers by embezzling their ticket payments. Emotions ran high when German authorities detained a group of Denver travelers because their tickets were not valid. We located the travel agent in England where he had fled, but technicalities in British law kept us from extraditing him back to Denver. He was so elated with that result that he took a trip to Hawaii to celebrate, whereupon he was arrested on a minor violation. We then were able to return him to Denver.

While in prison here, he made constant requests to the court for special food and privileges, based upon religious grounds. The last straw was his petition for a furlough to go to India to participate in a religious submersion in the Ganges River. The judge lost patience and released him to go to India for good.

The public is fascinated with the subject of prison escapes, a la James Cagney. In fact, most escapes are walk-aways by prisoners given special privileges because of their good prison conduct. Traditional escapes do occur. Once several inmates escaped from Denver County Jail by beating a hole in the wall with a set of barbells. When I asked a jailer how this could go undetected at the time, he explained that the guards thought the prisoners were just exercising with extra enthusiasm.

Prison officials are so paranoid about escapes and the resulting publicity that the Colorado Department of Corrections once issued a year-end statement proudly announcing that 98% of the inmates that year had *not* escaped.

Community corrections is the wave of the future in dealing with offenders who are not violent or serious enough to warrant penitentiary confinement, but who still require removal from society for a time. The typical community corrections sentence is for two years or less, at first in the County Jail and then in a halfway house. The offender spends each day on a regular job, or in school, but is confined on the weekends and at night.

In 1982, Denver district judges ordered 450 felony offenders into this program. After years of efforts, other counties began establishing similar programs and the legislature funded community corrections with relative generosity. It makes good financial sense, since it costs more to send a person to the penitentiary than to Harvard for a year.

Community corrections is not without its problems. My wife and I attended a play at the Gaslight Theater in Denver. To our surprise, the star actor was a man we had just convicted of robbing Denver Zoo officials of the proceeds from the Zoo's passenger train. He paraded around the stage with a pistol (part of the plot), in an excellent but seemingly long performance. The judge had sentenced the robber to community corrections. Instead of working each day and being locked up at night, he was locked up each day and released to his acting job in the evenings.

Corrections officials rarely miss the opportunity to use the particular talents of inmates. Before becoming district attorney, I once defended a certified public accountant who confessed to embezzlement. In prison, he became the warden's income tax return preparation expert.

Rick Carter was both a professional burgler/robber and a gourmet cook. He was transferred at an early date from the penitentiary to Bails Hall, a state-run halfway house in Denver. His cooking was excellent, but he spent most of his time running a burglary ring from his Bails Hall headquarters. His burglary business became so busy that he acquired an electronic beeper to keep him in touch with his operatives. When his activities became known, he escaped. We issued hundreds of wanted posters, identifying Carter as a gourmet cook. He was captured after his restaurant employer in a small town in Colorado turned him in. The employer said he regretted losing such a good cook.

Most people think prison terms are too short. So do I, for violent and career criminals. For garden variety offenders, the certainty of imprisonment is more important than the length. Many judges use what is called "shock probation," where an offender is sent to prison for a long term, then brought back to court within 120 days and placed on probation. For those to whom the shock of prison is a permanent deterrent, four months may do as much good as four years. For those who will return to their criminal ways, four years is not long enough.

A penal expert once said that a third of the prisoners will never again commit a crime, another third almost certainly will, and the other third may go either way. The difficulty is that we can't tell one third from another. Until we can, we should err on the side of caution and protection of society.

## Capital Punishment: Can Taking a Life Save Lives?

The only justification for capital punishment is deterrence, i.e., saving lives. Unfortunately, that central purpose is usually lost in the never-ending debate on the subject. Most often, proponents of the death penalty champion the cause of revenge, while opponents talk of the immorality of the state taking a life.

It is not possible to prove a negative, such as why certain crimes do not occur. Therefore, neither side is ever able to prove whether the presence of a viable death penalty means fewer murders. John Gilbert Graham blew up a United Airlines plane thirty years ago in a plot to collect on an insurance policy. No commercial airplane has been blown up in such circumstances since. Was Graham's execution a deterrent?

My belief is that in a narrow range of cases, capital punishment is a deterrent. However, one cannot take lightly the arguments of those who say that the state never has a right to take a life. Yet a leading opponent of the death penalty once admitted in a debate that it would have been morally right—even required—to kill Hitler to save the lives of six million Jews. Israel, with a national revulsion to the death penalty, made an exception when it executed Nazi mass murderer Adolph Eichmann. Almost everyone has a line beyond which the death penalty could apply. The debate should center on where to draw that line and whether there is any realistic prospect of the death penalty being generally permitted by the courts.

Voters in Colorado have repeatedly voted in favor of the death penalty. These same people, when called as prospective jurors in a death penalty case, overwhelmingly ask to be excused from service because of their unwillingness to return such a verdict. The specific case seems different from the general principle, they say. Some lawyers call that phenomenon hypocrisy. I view it more as a natural rethinking of an attitude when one is brought face-to-face with reality—plus a reluctance of some citizens to bear such a heavy responsibility.

Often repeated folklore is that murderers are good risks for rehabilitation because they don't kill again. My experience is that some of the worst murderers, the ones to whom capital punishment is most likely to be a deterrent, do kill again. A case in point is Joseph Corbett.

Corbett's mother died in a mysterious fall from an apartment building. Corbett was present, but there was no hard evidence that he killed her. Shortly thereafter, in California, he murdered an Air Force sergeant in a hitchhiking situation. He pleaded guilty to the murder and was sentenced to prison in California. He escaped and came to Colorado.

He next came to prominence when charged with the kidnapping murder of a member of the wealthy Coors family, owners of Adolph Coors Company of Golden, Colorado. The murder occurred on a lonely road, without witnesses. Therefore, there was legally no possibility of a death penalty when the jury found him guilty of murdering Coors. He was sentenced to life imprisonment, but was paroled after serving less than 18 years.

Our office fought the granting of the parole, but after a stormy hearing, it was granted anyway. True to our predictions, Corbett illegally left the state under an assumed name. We were able to revoke his parole, but not long after his return to prison he was paroled again. He served less time for his second murder conviction than most offenders do for their first.

Toby Lee Romero is another example of a repeat killer. After being convicted of one death, he brutally tortured and stabbed to death a young woman. We convicted him of first degree murder, but the jury was unable to agree on the death penalty, and Romero therefore received a life sentence. No one expects him to serve more than 20 years.

There are many other examples, but the point is clear: Not all murderers are good risks for rehabilitation because some killers do kill again. Society faces serious risks when such killers are released.

As in most states, Colorado's death penalty law is murky. The United States Supreme Court has contributed to the confusion. It first threw out death penalty laws for not having enough in the way of specific guidelines. When state legislatures responded by establishing strict guidelines, the Supreme Court threw the new laws out as being too rigid. Only time will tell if the latest generation of state capital punishment laws will pass constitutional muster.

Colorado's death penalty law is as narrow as any in the nation. It only applies to first degree murder cases if there is an aggravating factor (such as torture or contract murder). It never applies if there is any mitigating factor present (such as being under 18 years of age, or even if sane but being in an impaired mental state). In ten years, I sought the death penalty in only half a dozen cases, and then only where I felt the law clearly applied. Although those cases resulted in convictions, they did not result in death penalty sentences.

The last death penalty carried out in Colorado was in 1967. Louis Monge, defended by one of my former law partners, as court-appointed counsel, was executed for having murdered his wife and several of his children. There have been hundreds of murders in the state since then, but no executions. How can capital punishment be a deterrent when it is so rarely and unevenly applied?

Sound logic would say that if the death penalty is not in fact a deterrent because of its rare and uneven application, it ought to be replaced with a better deterrent. I began an effort to build support for a mandatory life sentence, without possibility of suspension, parole or commutation, to replace our death penalty statute. Under this proposal, the death penalty would be retained only for those who murder while serving a mandatory life sentence. There must always be a sanction, and another life sentence would be no deterrent to a life termer.

Despite the private support for this proposal, law enforcement and media leaders remain unwilling to advocate it publicly. "We agree with you, but are afraid we'd look soft on murder if we supported it openly," one editorial writer told me. My response went unanswered, "What is softer on murder than a penalty which, in practice, is no deterrent at all?"

# Chapter 18

# Criminal Justice Has Its Ironic Side

**Criminals**

For most crimes to occur, there must be both a criminal and a citizen/victim. Both actors are often bizzare in their actions. The following scenarios are merely representative of what goes on, week-in and week-out, in the criminal justice system.

There is a widespread public perception that a criminal is a careful, methodical, intelligent professional. That type of criminal is the exception rather than the rule. More typical is the burglar who broke into the Denver Wholesale Meat Company. He was captured as he was stealing boxes full of what he believed to be beef tenderloins. In fact, he was stealing boxes of beef rectums. At his trial, his fear seemed greater that his peers would learn of the stupidity of the crime than that he would be convicted. A smiling jury found him guilty after a very short deliberation.

But the classic example of the gang that couldn't shoot straight was the activist bombers' group who made Denver the bombing capitol of the nation in the 1970's. Several of its members apparently could not tell red wires from green ones, and blew themselves up in the process of planting bombs.

Several others placed a bomb in the back seat of a car in which they planned to drive to a district police station in Northwest Denver. Their plan was to blow up the station just as the annual convention of the International Chiefs of Police convened in Denver. Ever-mindful of details, the bombers started the timing device on the bomb as they began the drive to the police station target. Coincidentally, they were stopped by police officers en route. The police officers casually questioned the suspects while the bomb continued to tick in the back seat. Only this twist of fate caused the bomb to be detected and the timing device turned off before it exploded.

Crazy results are sometimes a product of the law. One criminal who benefited from a quirk in the law was shot in the buttock as he fled from a crime scene. The police officer who shot him had only a rear view of the suspect. Thus, the only positive identification of the escaped suspect was the bullet itself, which could be matched scientifically with the gun from which it was shot. When the suspect was later arrested, police found that the bullet was lodged more than an inch below the surface of the skin. Understandably, he declined the offer of an operation to remove the incriminating evidence. Case law prevented our obtaining a warrant for removal of the bullet, because it was more than a surface wound. Smiling but in pain, and not anxious to sit down, the suspect went free.

The spouse-killer is often the craziest of all. Most often, it is the husband who conspires to kill his wife. Such a case involved a prominent South Dakota businessman who decided that his divorce would be much less expensive if his wife were dead. He shared these ideas and his desire to engage a killer with a bartender in San Francisco known as Fat Freddy. Fat Freddy happened to be an FBI informant, and he cooperated in the ensuing investigation.

When the meeting between the husband and the apparent trigger man took place at Stapleton Airport in Denver, the coffee shop was alive with undercover law enforcement customers. When the wife's picture and a $5,000 down payment changed hands, the husband was quickly arrested. Upon pleading guilty to conspiracy to commit the crime, he was fined $25,000, an amount greater than the murder contract. The wife was irate over what she viewed as her husband's cheapness, as well as his plan to pay for the wicked deed in installments. Although he avoided prison, his divorce settlement became much more expensive.

Some criminals carefully increase the cost of their services based upon additional risks involved. Such a case involved Factual Services Bureau, Inc. That company had, for a quarter of a century and throughout the country, stolen—through subterfuge—confidential medical records. The firm's business was to sell the records to personal injury defense lawyers and insurance companies. The records were of immense value in defending medical claims. When this practice was reported to our office, we created an opportunity for the firm to steal the medical records of a member of our staff who happened to be in a Denver hospital. Upon learning the occupation of the patient, the firm raised the charge from $100 to $250, thereby bringing the offense up to a felony level. Their own greed helped us to put the firm out of business and to convict a number of its agents.

Some crooks have a warmth which can be surprising. One felony defendant, realizing that his defense was not going well, sprang to his feet in the courtroom and passionately kissed the most attractive woman in the jury. Predictably, the judge declared a mistrial. At least for that week, the defendant remained unconvicted.

Most people are surprised to learn of the generally warm reception which inmates later accord the prosecutors who convicted them. (The same is not true of defendants who are acquitted, who usually hold long grudges despite their good fortune.) Regularly, we took our staff to the penitentiary and to other correctional facilities as part of our in-service training program. Michael Borrelli (the convicted contract killer who was later acquitted in a retrial), left his post in the prison kitchen to talk to me as we were having lunch in the inmates' cafeteria. "If I had known you were coming down, I would have fixed you something special," he quipped with a smile.

A few minutes later appeared Juan Cortez, the career swindler we had convicted. He sat down to explain his new religious underpinnings, that he held no ill will ("You were just doing your job"), and to suggest that if we could help get him out, he would return forever to his native Texas. The "Great White Shark," as he liked to call himself, served his full minimum sentence.

And no audience was ever more courteous and attentive than when I addressed the Life Termers' Union at the state penitentiary.

### Citizens

I have always been surprised by the number of intelligent business people who are victimized by alchemist swindles. In one case, the victims were bankers who were persuaded to invest in a scheme in which the swindler promised he could turn lead into platinum. They finally reported the crime, but only after a long delay caused by their embarrassment and fear of public ridicule. True to his character, the defendant maintained that his system had actually worked. He said the heavy bar of platinum had been replaced with a heavy chunk of lead by a devious and very strong stewardess on a flight from Chicago to Denver.

An Irishman named O'Malley used the same scheme. He even swindled a number of victims after his well-publicized trial and conviction of just such a scam. He was able to continue his crimes (until he was eventually sentenced to prison) because the sentence for his first conviction was only a fine. The amount of the fine was several thousand dollars less than the fruits of the precious metals swindle of which he was convicted.

Some juries are reluctant to convict where the citizen/victim's gullibility rises to the level of stupidity. One such case was labeled by my deputy district attorneys as the "Failure to Swing" case. The defendant promised wild and extravagant sexual orgies to those who would leave their names and several hundred dollars in cash at a South Denver residence. The victims did their part, but the orgies never materialized. The felony theft by deception case was technically good, but the jury returned a verdict of not guilty. Left to their own desires, the jurors might well have convicted the erotic victims.

Few victims develop the rage of a business person victimized by a short check writer (or "paper hanger"). In addition to prosecuting fraud by check cases, we constantly encouraged businesses to exercise greater care in cashing checks. The most vivid example of failure to do so involved the cashing of a number of printed checks stolen from Howard Hardware Store. The thief successfully cashed the checks after signing each of them with the name "Howard Hardware."

We learned the hard way that whatever the suspected crime, when a citizen reports it, it deserves serious attention. One day a woman called to report that a barber shop in the Cherry Creek area was having nude women barbers give men regular haircuts for $25. When I replied, "That is an outrageous price for a regular haircut," the caller convinced me that being a smart alec was not what I was elected to be.

### The Process of Arrest

There is an inertia (in the physics sense) in criminal cases. The way they begin is often the way they continue, and what happens at the outset is often critical to being able to prove the case in court.

At trial, juries usually hear the details of the defendant's arrest. Sometimes those bring stifled smiles. One such case involved Roland Nocera, top executive of an illegal pyramid company called Holiday Magic, Inc. Nocera was resting in his hotel room, pants off, prior to his presentation of a major speech in the banquet room below. Our investigators appeared at his room with an arrest warrant. He tried to read the charges as he put on his trousers. His leaving the hotel in handcuffs surprised some of his executive officers and investors. He handled himself coolly until the car taking him to jail detoured to pick up the wife of one of my deputies who was attending a dance that evening. Nocera had only been in town a few hours, and as he sat handcuffed waiting for the dance partner to appear, he said to his captors (all of whom were in civilian clothes), "Are you guys really cops?"

The way in which a defendant handles himself at the time of arrest can affect the vigor with which the police put the case together. The Denver Police Department regularly conducted a decoy patrol. An undercover officer would pose as a bum asleep on the street, while other officers waited to capture those who would rob the decoy. The police unit had only a limited budget, but put $200 in marked bills in the pocket of the decoy officer. Once, as a thief took the money, the hidden officers swept down on him. The thief promptly put the $200 in his mouth and swallowed the evidence. The thief was convicted in a case in which the police took a particular and personal interest.

Before becoming district attorney, in my first trial as a lawyer by appointment, I defended Joe Nathan Clark. He was in need of better looking clothes for the trial, so I supplied him with my best tie, tie clasp and cuff links. I remember the case well, because after the jury convicted him of the drug charge, and as he was being taken from the courtroom with my additions to his wardrobe, my wife, who had watched the trial, was urging me to retrieve my property. I declined, and Clark left well-dressed to serve his time.

The next time I saw Clark was during a raid at The Hairdresser, an after-hours club. He greeted me warmly as I accompanied the police into the establishment. He insisted that I meet his friends, which I did while the officers waited to handcuff them and take them to jail. That was the last time I engaged in handshaking during a police action.

Generally, police officers welcome the opportunity to make an arrest and take someone to jail. The only time I saw that enthusiasm fail was on a Friday afternoon, the deadline for detectives to turn in their applications to take the sergeant's examination. That afternoon we were arresting and questioning a businessman whom the grand jury had just indicted for criminal extortion. He used collection methods which threatened the breaking of legs, and the grand jury took a dim view of such methods.

One by one, the detectives looked at their watches and excused themselves, until I was left alone with the suspect. Although I had watched him place his pistol in his desk drawer, I was less than comfortable in driving him, otherwise alone, to the police station. As I discharged him from my custody he said, "Thanks for the ride. When this is all over, we ought to get together for lunch." He pleaded guilty and I passed on the lunch.

### The Suspects are Best at Solving the Crime

Herb Berger, president of Mutual Graphics, Inc., received a call from a man offering to sell unpublished telephone numbers and names for 25 cents per name. Because of the numbers involved, Berger knew it was big and illegal business. He called and we had him arrange a meeting, which we recorded. The seller was arrested. We wanted not only to convict the defendant, but to learn how this serious breach of Mountain Bell's security system could occur.

The defendant agreed to plead guilty if we would not object to his leaving the state. We agreed, provided that he would disclose the obviously ingenious way in which he had penetrated the security of Colorado's largest employer. He and his lawyer met us at a downtown coffee shop at 2 a.m. Together we walked down an alley. The defendant was then greeted by two Mountain Bell maintenance men, who shouted, "Bill, good to see you. Do you need some more of that unshredded paper for your hog pens?"

The Fencing Unit of the Police Department, under our legal supervision, conducted a storefront operation in which undercover officers posed as purchasers of stolen goods. The transactions were filmed on a hidden camera and were recorded. A professional burgler named White talked himself into possibly a longer prison term when, on tape, he explained to the undercover officers that he was a specialist.

"I do business burglaries, not home burglaries," he explained. "The reason is that for a business burglary, you only face an indeterminate sentence, but for a home burglary, you can get 5 to 40 years. That's why I'm a specialist."

Rules of evidence are designed to admit reliable testimony. That which occurs at stressful times is often considered in the law to be particularly reliable. One such rule is the dying declaration rule. It says that if a person thinks he is dying, he won't go to his Maker with a lie on his lips, and that his dying declarations are therefore considered truthful. Kelvin Booker disproved that legal principle.

Booker was shot in the jaw by an off-duty Denver police officer. As he thought he was dying, he said from his stretcher that the shot was fired by a stranger in a black jacket, not the officer. At the hospital, when Booker was told he would recover, he then told the truth and identified the officer, as had the other witnesses. Practice is often different from theory.

Experienced thieves are also more skillful than amateurs. We investigated reports that Regional Transportation District bus drivers were stealing as much as $100 a week from the fare boxes on the buses. We placed investigators on the suspect buses, and these riders deposited marked money. At the end of the day, when some of the marked money was not among the receipts, we knew we had the right targets. The investigation was fruitful and a number of drivers were charged and pleaded guilty.

One experienced driver demanded a trial. At trial, our prosecutor engaged in a courtroom demonstration with one of the fare boxes, illustrating how money went into the box and how it was later retrieved. The deputy placed a dollar in the box. It disappeared. No one could find it in the box. The fare box ate another dollar bill as the jury smiled and even our prosecutor could not keep a straight face. The jury found the experienced driver not guilty, but did so with a smile.

Arrests and proving how a crime was committed are one thing. Proving each and every element of a crime beyond a reasonable doubt to a jury of twelve citizens can be something else again.

## Chapter 19

# The Role of Prejudice, Discrimination and Ethnicity

Just as surely as discrimination exists in our society, it exists in our system of justice. It shouldn't, but it does. Even though a majority of those in prison in Colorado are Anglos, a disproportionate number are from the Black and Hispanic communities. The irony is that Blacks and Hispanics more often are victims of crime than are Anglos.

There are a number of reasons for this situation. Those who commit street crimes are more likely to be caught than those who commit white collar or complex crimes. Proportionately, more street crime offenders come from the lower economic levels, where there are more minorities. Finally, our society often discriminates in jobs, housing and treatment of minorities generally. The fact is that a minority youth picked up by the police has a better chance of being taken to Juvenile Hall than a juvenile from an affluent area, who may simply be taken home to his parents. Even with all of that, the overwhelming majority of those who grow up ill-housed, ill-clothed, and poorly educated also grow up as law abiding citizens.

### Our Race Relations History is Not a Proud One

Denver and Colorado do not have a proud history in race relations. The Ku Klux Klan controlled the Colorado House of Representatives in the 1920's, when Klansmen prepared the jury lists in Denver and elected Judge Morley as their Klan-member governor.

The Klan-type bias is alive in Colorado, but it is now less visible. That influence can still create violence. One fall day, a young Black man, Melvin Meadows, took his white girlfriend to a movie at U-Hills Cinema. A stranger came into the darkened theater, sat down beside Meadows and shot him in the head, killing Meadows instantly. The gunman then left the theater and killed himself. A later search of the assailant's apartment produced a stock of the racist and hate literature typically pushed by the KKK.

We followed closely the increased Klan activities. David Duke, Grand Dragon, announced that he was coming to Denver. This was shortly after he was indicted in Louisiana for conspiring to incite a riot. Violence always seemed to follow in his path. Public officials are constantly welcoming people to their communities. I decided to "unwelcome" Duke, and wrote a letter to him to that effect. He arrived in Denver before my letter caught up with him, so I called him into my office to unwelcome him personally. That created some furor, and an entire centerfold in *The Crusader*, the national KKK newspaper, criticizing my actions. But Duke didn't return to Denver.

During the next several days, we received considerable harassment. A fire truck arrived at our home in response to a false alarm. The next day, police with guns drawn came to our house to handle a "violent scene," another false report. On the third day my wife, Mary Ann, received a call asking if I was allergic to any drugs.

"Why do you ask?" she inquired.

"Because your husband has been taken to the hospital with a serious heart attack," responded the caller.

It took 45 minutes before Mary Ann determined that the caller was an impostor and the report was a false one. I was attending a luncheon meeting at the time. While we couldn't prove all these calls were Klan-initiated, I have no doubt of it.

Suddenly hate literature was being widely distributed at night in Denver, much of it KKK materials. We determined that much of the actual delivery was being done by the American Nazi Party. We developed two informants within that organization. The group was not particularly well organized, but I was surprised that so many of its members were young people. They felt economically and educationally threatened by the upward progress of minorities. Our monitoring efforts, together with good work by the Police Intelligence Unit and the Anti-Defamation League, seemed to stop the problem—but not the bigotry which began and sustains such movements.

Since before the turn of the century, Colorado has had a law prohibiting discrimination in public accommodations. But we found that many of the discos operating in the Denver area had begun to discriminate openly. Some of the establishments kept Blacks out by discriminatory enforcement of dress codes. Blue jeans were permitted for Whites, but not Blacks. Others required double picture identification for minorities. One establishment even marked its music tapes with white dots on those tapes which they believed Blacks would not enjoy. The disc jockey was instructed to play those tapes when several Blacks had gained admission. The pattern was broken, but not before a bomb exploded at one disco at the height of the discrimination.

Discrimination is not limited to racial minorities. One afternoon an irate blind person called. Along with his seeing eye dog, he was being denied admission to a Denver movie theater. We advised the theater manager that it would be illegal to deny them admission, and they were then admitted.

At the time, I was curious as to why a blind person would want to go to a movie. A year later I hired Dana Wakefield, the first blind prosecutor in Colorado history (and now an outstanding Denver Juvenile Court judge). He explained how important it is for a blind person to attend such events and to be fully in the mainstream of activities. Judge Dana regularly attends the Denver Broncos football games.

In truth, it was the progressiveness of our staff rather than my own that caused us to hire Wakefield. I was at first reluctant because we were dealing with public funds for salaries, and I was uncertain if a blind person could overcome his handicap in court. The staff said he could, and we hired him—but only on a probationary basis and for less than he should have been paid. We later provided him a reader, and he became one of our finest chief deputies. Years later I was to learn that in those early months, he worked nights selling goods door-to-door to make ends meet. The lesson is that discrimination can be as much a product of caution as of design.

Just as we made a conscious effort not to discriminate in cases based upon race, creed or color, we made the same effort with regard to the handicapped. One target of our prosecution was a wheelchair cripple who had become proficient at second story burglaries. Another wheelchair defendant, Roger Moore, we tried and convicted of murdering his roommate, cutting the body into pieces, placing parts of it in the refrigerator and delivering arms and legs around the neighborhood. He was captured as he was about to board a plane for Chicago, his roommate's hands carefully tucked in his luggage.

Traditionally, women defendants have received preferential treatment and women lawyers have been the objects of discrimination. Both may be changing as there are more women lawyers and more women defendants. Still, women commit proportionately fewer crimes than men, and most male judges have a well-known reluctance to send women to prison.

At an early date, I learned not to jest with feminists on this issue. I was confronted at the District Attorney's Building by several leaders of the Denver Chapter of the National Organization of Women. They were alarmed that, in one day, we had not yet captured a kidnapper of two young women. In that setting, I quipped, "You make a good point about the unequal treatment of women. I just left the County Jail, where today there were 600 male inmates and only 20 women. We've got to convict more women to even up those numbers." They saw little humor in my comments, and picketed my office.

The solution to discrimination lies in actions, not words, and in full involvement of minorities, women and the handicapped in positions of authority. The staff I took over when I became district attorney had only one Black, one Hispanic, and one woman prosecutor—and no women investigators. The staff I turned over to my successor 10 years later was composed of women and minorities at every level. Half of the lawyers were minorities and women and one-third of the investigators were women. In fact, women headed half a dozen units within the office.

It is that process of upward mobility which creates both the fact and the appearance of equal treatment. Our generation will deserve harsh judgment for not tapping fully the talents of our women and minority communities. We will deserve even harsher judgment if we now falter in moving toward a solution.

### Ethnicity

In a shrinking world, one of every five Denver citizens is either foreign-born or has at least one foreign-born parent. The same then must be true of those who violate the law. While ethnic generalities can be erroneous and overstated, still subcultures do influence their members in unique ways.

According to the 1980 Census, Asian-Americans in Denver have the highest per capita income of any group. They are generally thrifty and law abiding. Their family structures tend to be strong, and peer pressure and maintaining respect are powerful influences to obey the law.

Some members of the Korean community saved their money and bought a number of motels on East Colfax Avenue. For a time, prostitution became so active that prostitutes openly used walkie-talkies on Colfax to warn one another of approaching police officers. They would take their customers (called in street talk "Johns" or "Marks") to Colfax motels. We closed one motel and then called on owners of others, asking that they stop renting to known prostitutes, or face similar action.

One Korean owner simply could not understand my request. I told him no more "prostitutes, hookers, women selling sex, ladies of the night." Still he shook his head, not understanding. The chief deputy accompanying me finally spoke up.

"No more business women," he warned.

"Oh! OK," said the Korean. "Not like Seoul." We never had another complaint about the motel.

State Wildlife officers asked that we prosecute some Korean-Americans for fishing with large nets in Denver lakes. "Did you first tell them that net fishing isn't allowed here?" I asked. They said they had not warned them, but would reluctantly do so, even though "it would do no good." The fishermen didn't know such fishing was illegal, and after that warning, they never again fished with nets, as they had in Korea.

Other Asian-American communities are equally law-abiding. In 1972, the Organized Crime Unit during my predecessor's administration raided an annual Chinese New Years party. Dozens of leading members of the community were arrested for illegal gambling. Their names were printed in the paper, a great affront to them and their families. The cases were never prosecuted because the police could never understand the games, much less prove that they were illegal games of chance. Six months later, the legislature legalized gambling incidental to bona fide social relationships.

The Arab community retains a certain eye-for-an-eye tradition. We had begun an investigation into a number of Arab-owned grocery stores which were selling wormy and infected foods. We obtained appropriate court orders against the stores. Soon thereafter an Arab store owner was found stabbed to death in his bathtub. Word in the community was that he had been an informant in our investigation. In fact, he had not been. Two people from a competing Arab store confessed to the murder, then both recanted. The bottom line was that we were never able to prove who committed the murder, so no case could be pursued in court.

One day a member of the Jordanian embassy appeared in my office to say that unless we filed a case against a suspected killer, the Arabs' code would permit the victim's family to kill a member of the suspect's family, or demand as much as $25,000 in reparations.

"That code and tradition cannot apply here," I warned the diplomat.

"No matter," he said. "This tradition applies throughout the world."

We provided endless affidavits to the Jordanian government explaining why no case could be filed, and finally dissuaded the grieving family from seeking revenge—at least in Denver.

On another occasion, a Saudi Arabian student became involved in a pool hall argument with a young Denver man. The Saudi attacked the young man as he left the pool room, and was struck on the head with a pool cue in return. The Saudi later died from the blow. We filed murder charges, but dismissed them after a lengthy preliminary hearing when it became clear that the defendant had acted in self-defense. However, the Saudi was the son of a close friend of the King of Saudi Arabia. Suddenly a Texas law firm hired by the Saudis appeared, demanding that the case be refiled. We refused. Only after months of federal litigation and decisions upholding our dismissal did the Saudis abandon their fight for refiling of a clearly unjust murder charge.

South and Central American justice often depends more on who is the defendant than what is the crime. Following a Medicaid fraud investigation, we filed multiple felony counts of double-billing against a Chilean psychiatrist, Dr. Carlos Worter. Just before trial, he jumped bond. We located him in Santiago, where he enjoyed an influential relationship with his government. Despite a long-established extradition treaty with Chile, the

Chilean government refused to consider his extradition to Denver. In absentia, through his Denver lawyer, he pleaded guilty to the charges as misdemeanors and repaid the $45,000 he had received from his illegal billings. It was the best we could do, given the refusal of the Chilean government to honor the rule of law.

By contrast, Costa Rica, a Central American country with the strongest tradition of democracy, readily returned an embezzler to Denver. In fact, that government sent law officers deep into the interior on horseback to capture and return the criminal to Colorado.

Perhaps the most frightening view of South of the Border justice came while I was talking by telephone with the police chief of a small Mexican town. The chief had in custody a suspect who critically wounded a man in Denver and then fled to Mexico.

"What do you want him to confess to?" the chief asked. I told the chief in no uncertain terms that he was not to talk with or abuse the prisoner in any way. We quickly arranged to bring the prisoner back to Denver, where he was found guilty without need of any evidence of a confession.

**Europeans, Too**

European immigrants have provided their fair share of offenders and problems. A Czech named Vesely filed in one year more than thirty state income tax returns in order to receive, illegally, the $24 per person state sales tax refund on each return. During the investigation, he and his wife spoke excellent English. As soon as he was arrested, he shouted, "You Nazis. You are going to shoot me." Those were his last words in English. He wanted a Czech judge, a Czech lawyer, a Czech jury and everything but a Czech sentence. He received a Czech interpreter for the trial, an American guilty verdict and a Denver sentence.

Greek immigrants have a particular pride. We convicted George Vlahos of criminal conspiracy in connection with the robbery and killing of a Greek restaurant owner named Armatas. The robbers took Armatas' wallet and coins, but failed to look in his front pocket, in which he was carrying $1,200 in cash. Reportedly, Vlahos was more despondent over failing to take the $1,200 than over his conviction and sentence.

A case involving phony Russian rubles illustrates what an

interdependent world it is. Two Soviet immigrants came to Denver and swindled a number of Soviet Jewish immigrants through the sale of phony rubles. Before they could be arrested, the swindlers fled. They were discovered in Greece. These Soviet swindlers of Jewish victims in Denver were extradited from Greece to the United States through the efforts of a deputy sheriff of Italian descent and our extradition specialist named Kennedy.

*Chapter 20*

# Dimensions of the District Attorney's Role

**Running the Show**

Harry Truman was right when he said that the buck stops at the top. He could have added that how well the buck is handled depends mostly on the quality of the people selected by the buck-stopper. Good management means managing by exception—letting the best qualified people make most of the decisions.

A little-recognized reason for hiring the best possible people is that the person doing the hiring is most influenced by the people surrounding him—those very people. In picking the right people, it is important to follow your own instincts.

We were about to hire six trial investigators. Our office screening committee made recommendations to me, and I met the top six candidates before they were hired. We expected that my meeting them would be mostly a formality. After meeting the top-rated prospect, I told him we would be "back in touch." We hired the other five, but something I couldn't put my finger on bothered me about the top applicant. I told the staff to check him out further.

With reluctance they rechecked his references, and he checked out superbly. He had held responsible positions and seemed to be well acquainted with the system in the East, where he had lived. I called him back and offered him the job, which he eagerly accepted. The staff was delighted that I had seen the error of my concern, but as I offered the position to him, some instinct told me I was making a mistake.

The next day, quite fortuitously, we learned that he was a phony, had assumed false credentials and was even under investigation in the Denver suburbs for practicing law without a license. When I called to tell him why he would not be hired after all, he said, "Oh, well, it was worth a try." I then vowed always to follow my own instincts. If a mistake is to be made, better that it be your own than someone else's.

No one bats a thousand in personnel decisions. Sometimes you simply make a mistake. Other times the job itself may change or the person hired may change or run out of gas. Therefore, part of running the show is recognizing these situations and humanely terminating an appointee as soon as the need is clear.

When I took office, we hired increasing numbers of attorneys from prestigious law firms, a complete reversal of the historical experience in the office. That was due more to the policy of delegation of authority than to increased salaries.

Giving appointees the right to be wrong carries with it substantial risk, but on balance it is well worth it. Our view was that if a deputy district attorney could decide the fate of a murder case, he ought to be able to decide what to say to the press. Our press relations policy was simple. No one was either gagged or required to talk with the media. The lawyers knew what they could and could not say about a case under the Code of Professional Responsibility, and they were instructed either to tell the truth or give no comment.

I had always taken a dim view of bigamy cases. I consider them essentially noncriminal, low priority matters. The staff knew we wouldn't file them. However, one swindler, in the midst of his swindle trial, married a second wife (a victim of his swindles) before divorcing the first. He obviously was seeking both jury sympathy and a more cooperative witness. The deputy trying the case was so outraged that he told a reporter that the defendant should be prosecuted for bigamy. He added: "But Dale says it will be a cold day in hell before we file a bigamy case. That's off the record."

The quote appeared in the press. It was accurate, although obviously not off the record. We didn't file the bigamy case, and took some criticism from those who felt I was "soft on bigamy." That criticism was a small price to pay for an environment in which staff members were considered responsible enough to deal with the media without interference.

For some reason, public officials are more reluctant to admit mistakes than nearly anyone else. That weakness brought the Viet Nam downfall to President Johnson and the Watergate scandal to President Nixon. It took me a number of years to learn the basic lesson that if the office had goofed, everyone is better served with a candid admission of the mistake, rather than by stonewalling tactics.

The District Court required us to file charges against a suspect in jail within three working days after his arrest, or the suspect would be released. In a garden variety felony case, we failed to meet that deadline. A newspaper reporter got wind of it and called me for an explanation. "We simply fouled up," I said. "We're going to tighten up on our procedures so that hopefully this kind of thing won't happen again."

There was only a small story about the error in the next day's press. I later learned that the reporter and his city editor had planned a major expose on the foul-up, but what news value was there with an admission rather than a denial of responsibility or finger-pointing?

One of the most important, most interesting and most trying aspects of being in elective office is dealing with the public. We adopted a Citizens' Afternoon program, during which (at a prescribed time at least monthly) any citizen could come in or call in and talk privately with me, without prescreening or a prior appointment. Although the staff referred to these as "Kook Sessions," I quickly learned their value.

At one of the first sessions, an elderly man came into my office, closed the door, and said he had a confession to make. I properly advised him of his right to remain silent, but he insisted. He explained that, 30 years before, he had taken a woman friend from Denver to Cheyenne, Wyoming, and had spent the night with her. He said he knew he had violated the Mann Act by transporting a woman across state lines for immoral purposes. When I told him that the statute of limitations had long since run on any such violation, and that it would not have been prosecuted anyway, he exploded with relief, "I can sleep again, for the first time in 30 years."

The greatest challenges come from people with competing and strongly-held views. Frances was a young adult who chose to join the Hare Krishna religious sect. Her father, a pipefitter from New Jersey, and her mother came to Denver to rescue their daughter. They secured a court order and deputy sheriffs set out to find Frances.

I was called to the scene when the deputy sheriffs and the

Hare Krishna leaders came to a standoff. The religious group members were hiding Frances and the lawmen were threatening to kick down all the doors in the 1400 block of Cherry Street to find her. Every available television crew was recording the escalating incident. After several hours of shuttle diplomacy, all parties agreed that Frances would be placed in my custody.

When I called my wife and told her that "we" had temporary custody of a 22-year-old member of the Hare Krishna sect, Mary Ann quickly corrected me. " 'You' have custody of her," she said. We arranged to pick up the special food she required and kept her whereabouts secret from her parents. We finally persuaded the parents to recognize that they could not legally prevent Frances from following her own lifestyle, even if they considered it wrong.

Several years later I ran into Frances at Stapleton Airport in Denver where, in full Hare Krishna regalia, she was spreading the word and literature of her group.

"How are your parents taking all this now?" I asked.

"Much better," she replied. "Mother is in Denver for a while and is living at our temple."

Public office is not that much different from private responsibility. Running the show is setting the tone and the priorities, picking and keeping the best people, dealing candidly with the public and the media, delegating authority and, most important, staying out of the way when the show is running well.

**Elect or Appoint the District Attorney?**

Well-motivated, experienced people disagree on whether the best public officials are chosen by election or by appointment. If independence of action and accountability to the public are keystones of good government, as I believe they are, then the elective system provides them with far more certainty than does an appointive process. The public's remedy of removing an inadequate public servant at the polls can be swift and clearly understood. That some good people would not submit themselves to the electorate is a small price to pay for the benefits of independence, accountability and removability.

Our decisions on whom to investigate, prosecute or not prosecute were never subjected to outside approval. The only time that occurs is when the prosecutor serves in an appointive system.

We investigated, and the grand jury indicted for securities fraud, the head of one of the largest churches in America. The principal defendant, Pastor Charles E. Blair, was and still is one of Denver's most popular religious leaders. Before trial, a group of prominent civic and business leaders called on me, urging that we drop the case.

"God does not want this case prosecuted," one of them said.

"With all due respect, God is not a party to this lawsuit. It is the People of the State of Colorado vs. Charles E. Blair," I answered.

The case went to trial and the jury found Blair guilty, after which the court placed him on probation so that he could better be in a position to make restitution.

By contrast, U.S. Attorneys serve by appointment and must secure Washington approval in major cases. A good example is the case of John M. King, flamboyant former head of King Resources. We had begun an investigation of King about the same time the U.S. attorney began looking into his questionable activities. Having both state and federal grand juries investigating the same acts at the same time can often cause problems. To try to avoid those conflicts, we met with the then-U.S. Attorney. We agreed to hold our investigation in abeyance on the condition that the federal investigation proceed in earnest, without delay and without influence. We knew that King had a close association with President Nixon, who was then in office. The U.S. Attorney agreed and the federal probe continued while we waited, as agreed.

Our statute of limitations on King's major activities would expire in 1974, and we expressed concern about the time the federal investigation was consuming.

"No cause for concern," we were told.

Then, John King announced his candidacy as an independent for the U.S. Senate seat then held by Sen. Peter Dominick, who was seeking reelection. Insider speculation was that his announcement was done to make it difficult for a Republican administration to prosecute him during the campaign, since it might look political and could hurt Sen. Dominick's reelection chances.

Our worst fears were realized. In rapid succession the federal probe in Colorado died amid speculation that Washington had put it on hold, and our statute of limitations expired. (Later, King was convicted on a smaller portion of his activities by a federal jury in New York, and he served a short prison sentence.) After that experience, I vowed never again to rely on the assurances of an appointed prosecutor, where the commitments made could be overruled by his boss.

The elective system is what Winston Churchill called the worst form of government, except for all the rest. Elections take their toll on the public, the candidates, their families and their supporters. They are long and expensive, and the news media are having an increasing impact on the outcome of elections.

Before Watergate, reporters generally reported what each candidate said and left to the readers and viewers the interpretation of those events. The Watergate era wrought fundamental changes in journalism's standard in the reporting of campaigns. Reporters now are deeply immersed in the mechanics of the campaign, often at the expense of the substance of the issues. Newspaper reporters, in particular, engage in interpretive reporting, complete with adjectives and conclusions which only a few years ago would have been reserved for the editorial pages.

A former newspaper editor, in lamenting this trend, has told me that much of the blame rests with new technology. He explained that in years past, a hard-nosed city editor could make substantial changes in obviously-slanted stories, using a trusted pencil. Now, stories are written on computer screens. Although the technology is available to city editors to edit stories, strike biased conclusions and remove editorial comment, that is done much less frequently now than when editors used pencils because it is more complicated.

The final evidence in support of our elective system over all others is that, even with its faults and problems, in 10 years no person tried to bribe me or a member of the staff. No campaign supporter received special treatment. In fact, my former campaign manager, a lawyer, stopped representing clients charged with crimes in Denver because the trial deputies bent over backwards to be sure that his clients received vigorous treatment. In most countries, those who hold elective office would not abide such behavior.

### Unintended Consequences

What I came to call the District Attorney's Law of Unintended Consequences is not limited to that office. It applies to the decision-making process generally. Simply stated, most decisions result in consequences which are unintended and usually unforeseen. They may have a more far-reaching impact than the original purpose of the decision ever anticipated. While most decision-makers try to be open-minded in reaching a decision, they often forget to look for unexpected by-products.

This entire concept first came to mind when we were facing a growing volume of street traffic in methadone. Methadone is an addictive, opiate-based substitute for heroin. Because it does not produce the same highs and lows as heroin, designated clinics are allowed to supply it to heroin addicts to permit them some normalcy in life. Addict patients were allowed to take home up to a week's supply of methadone, but there was good evidence that much of this was being sold on the illicit drug market.

I insisted on new standards which sharply reduced the amount and extent of the take-home privileges. The decision was a controversial one at first, among both patient/addict groups and with staff members of the drug treatment clinics.

The change had the intended result. We didn't again face as much street traffic in methadone. However, the most important results were a surprise—a positive surprise. The requirement of more frequent trips to the clinics greatly improved the quality of treatment. Medical experts have since confided that they found out that patients never had needed as much methadone as they had provided.

Unexpected negative results can as easily occur. Well-intended, overprotective parents, in an effort to maintain a close family relationship with their children, often cause the children to withdraw further from the family. That was the end result when Denver parents of Greek background hired nationally-known cult deprogrammer Ted Patrick to kidnap their adult daughters and "deprogram" them. The parents were convinced that their daughters were under the influence of a witch and her son. We never found any evidence of that. Instead, it appeared that the independent young women simply chose a lifestyle unfamiliar and totally unacceptable to their traditional parents.

The young women were captured as they left work and were taken forcibly to a cabin in Eldorado Springs, northwest of Denver. There, they were the subject of shouting, railing and restraint. Then they were taken to San Diego, California, and kept locked in a house until we managed to locate and free them. We brought Patrick back to Denver for prosecution. After a long and emotional trial, which further alienated the parents from their daughters, the jury found Patrick guilty of false imprisonment, for which he served a year in Denver County Jail. The parents pleaded no contest to the same false imprisonment charges and were given probation on the condition that they not interfere again in their daughters' lives. The young women successfully sued their own parents to restrain them from repeating the kidnapping and interference—all the precise opposite of what the parents had set out to achieve.

Oftentimes, unintended consequences can be anticipated and avoided. The Atlantis Community is an organization of disabled people who have consistently sought better public transportation for the handicapped. One day, its members chained their wheelchairs to the stairway of the Regional Transportation District (RTD) office building, to protest the RTD's refusal to provide more handicapped-accessible buses.

Both RTD and police commanders wanted us to prosecute these disabled citizens for criminal trespass. We declined, because we knew the unintended consequences would have been more protests, a raucous trial and creation of the very platform for their protests which prompted their actions in the first place. The problem was better handled through a civil restraining order, which is precisely what happened.

Even the results of well-planned and expensive reforms often surprise their advocates. That happened repeatedly with the billions of dollars granted by the federal Law Enforcement Assistance Administration (LEAA) to state and local criminal justice agencies. Our office worked hard to receive, and spend well, more than two million dollars of LEAA funds—more than was received by any other prosecutor's office in the Rocky Mountain region. In every case, these funds supported programs which we otherwise would have financed anyhow through local funds. That was a consequence opposite of that which Washington intended—to support worthy projects which would otherwise perish due to lack of funding.

We were not alone. This went on all over the country until, billions of dollars later, Congress finally caught on and abolished LEAA. Congress had failed to realize that state and local officials would almost always seek federal funds to ease pressures on their own funding sources.

Our Whistlestop/Neighborhood Watch crime prevention program was the most successful in the country. More than 110,000 Denverites (more than one in five) left their homes to attend block and neighborhood meetings to pursue neighborhood crime prevention. It had the intended result of crime reduction. The number of burglaries actually dropped in Denver between 1972 and 1982.

However, there were even more important unanticipated benefits. The program got neighbors together, sometimes for the first time. Often a new sense of neighborhood was established. The police officers regularly assigned to the neighborhood attended these meetings, and the citizens and police talked with one another face-to-face, often for the first time. Complaints about police conduct fell sharply, we believe as an unexpected consequence of this program.

We established a student jury system, whereby student peers of nonviolent juvenile offenders decided the punishment (within established, legal guidelines). One of my own teenage children initially opposed it as an "unworkable idea," and one of the daily newspapers editorially termed it "wrongheaded." In fact, it enjoyed great success and has become a national model. It achieved its intended purpose of rehabilitating youthful offenders. Fewer than ten percent again ran afoul of the law.

It had two even more important, unexpected consequences.

First, it had a particularly powerful impact on the families of the offenders. An example is a case in which the student jury called in the father of a young shoplifter. In no uncertain terms they took the father to task for not giving more support to his son, and for "cutting him down and always calling him 'short.'" The father was devastated, but he shaped up.

Second, hundreds of students who have served on student juries describe the service as one of their most important learning experiences. Either of these two results alone would have justified beginning the program.

In summary, few decisions have the precise consequences intended. Almost all have important unintended consequences, some positive, some negative. Inventors long ago learned this lesson and learned also to keep an open mind and to follow up on surprise by-products. That is a lesson all of us and our institutions ought to learn.

## Conclusions

During a decade as district attorney, my office prosecuted more than 200,000 cases. We established new standards for the decent treatment of victims and witnesses, the forgotten people in our criminal justice system.

We initiated and pushed for reforms of the system, from police priorities to the conduct of Grand Juries, and from corrections to sentencing practices. Along the way we lost a few battles which we should have won—battles which one day my successors will win. These include reform of our archaic bail bond system, elimination of unwarranted delays of justice, and making our system more a search for the truth than a complex procedural game.

As I reflect on those ten years and that staff which daily faced violence and the dark side, I am amazed that they could keep their idealism and abiding optimism in the human spirit. Our duty was first and foremost to seek justice. Hopefully, that was our most lasting contribution. In any event, I'd rather be district attorney in Denver then anywhere else in the world.

# VII

# EPILOGUE

Dale and Mary Ann gathered the family together for a portrait early in 1983, as the final mayoralty campaign was beginning. The young Tooleys left to right, are Brian, Kyla, Patrick and Keith.

# Chapter 21

# Cancer and Hope

*While addressing a men's group shortly after his cancer diagnosis, Dale was asked about his philosophy in dealing with a terminal illness. He quoted Winston Churchill during the darkest days of the Blitz in London during World War II. When asked by a group of young soldiers what advice he would give them, Churchill replied, "Never, never, never give in."*

*Dale Tooley's human spirit never gave in. He believed that tenacity brought hope, if not for himself at least for other cancer patients who would someday conquer the disease.*

*This message became the foundation for the Project of Hope—Spring 1985—to benefit the American Cancer Society's Residential Crusade. As a major part of this crusade, Dale agreed to "go public" with his illness.*

*His candor would become a vehicle for reaching out to others suffering from cancer—to share with them his sense of hope.*

*Never was there an expression of bitterness or regret about his pending death. He accepted it totally as life's random selection process.*

— **Jean Galloway**

All my life, I had operated under the philosophy that the human body is like an automobile: as long as it is running, don't mess it up. Every time I ever took my car in for a tuneup, it became tempermental and needed repairs. I tried the same approach with my body, and it worked great for 51 years. However, in the fall of 1984, Mary Ann finally persuaded me, after five years, to have a routine physical. I did so on

November 27.

It became apparent from the eyes of Dr. Jeffrey Houston that there was a serious problem in my belly and with my liver. The following week I underwent comprehensive tests at University Hospital, and on December 5 Mary Ann and I met with Dr. John Singleton, our longtime friend and expert University Hospital physician.

"The news is bad," he said, in what proved to be an understatement. The liver was badly extended by malignant cancer throughout, and it was not operable. There was a serious question of whether any treatment would be effective, and it was not certain just how much time I would have. Another test, a liver biopsy, was scheduled the following day. Mary Ann and I had a cup of coffee in a state of shock.

We called each of our children at the University of Colorado. We said, "We don't have many command performances, but we're going to have one this Friday. Sorry to interrupt your studies, but it will take a couple of hours. Please come for dinner." They pressed us for the reason for this suspicious and unique command performance, but we only told them that they would find the subject matter "of great interest." Advising the children was the toughest part of the entire process. We didn't want to interrupt their studies, but we knew the fact of my having cancer would soon reach the press, and we could not risk their learning of it from the newspapers.

Unknown to us, they all arrived at our house on Thursday and stayed overnight. Mary Ann and I, meanwhile, were at Rose Memorial Hospital and although the children called most hospitals, they missed that one. They didn't know whether the news was good or bad, although they suspected the worst, and they didn't know whether the problem was with Mary Ann or with me.

On Friday, December 7 (appropriately, Pearl Harbor Day), we bought Chinese food and sat down over a meal with the children. I was to be the only one who ate the food. I wanted to discuss the problem frankly and openly with the children, but despite the two thousand speeches I had given, I didn't know if I could handle this one without breaking down. Therefore, I prepared a letter to each of them which I asked them to read and which we discussed fully after they had done so. It is worth setting out the letter in full, because it describes my sentiments then and now:

December 7, 1984

To Our Magnificent Children:

The bad news is that I have cancer. While it is not operable, it may (to an extent not yet determined) be treatable. You can bet I'll do my best to lick it, but you deserve to know it is very much an uphill battle. (I'm sorry to tell you this just before your final exams, but there was no way to delay it, and you deserve the truth.)

Now the good news, which is much longer. Mary Ann and I have four magnificent children, and two wonderful additions to our family with Beth and Lori. My love for each of you is total and unconditional. Beyond loving you, which I haven't told you often enough, I *like* you!

In only 51 years, I have already lived the equal of many full lives. No one could have a better marriage than ours, nor a more perfect wife than Mary Ann. Together, we have engaged in the right causes and, I believe, jointly maintained the right values. Who could ask for more? Don't let anything in your own lives get in the way of that most important relationship, your marriage.

I want to repeat that we're going to do our best to whip this problem, but everyone at some point faces death. It comes with the territory. It is a natural part of the process of life. Most people never have the opportunity I now seize to deal with it with you, together, as a loving family. For all of this I am truly blessed.

Now, some ground rules:

1) This session tonight is the *only* command performance!

2) As I said, I both love and like each of you, in part because of the great way you have treated Mary Ann and me. If you now begin to treat us differently, we are not going to like it. So treat us the same as always and let's keep this great relationship, come what may.

**3) I will be mighty unhappy if you change your lives or lifestyles as a result of my problem. If what you most want to do is in New York or California or Broken Bow (well, maybe not Broken Bow), do it.**

**4) Finally, all this business with my belly is not a taboo subject. It is an inevitable subject. I want you neither to avoid nor to dwell on it. Treat it as the natural subject and process which it is. We'll have plenty of time to talk. There will be some emotion (which is one reason I have put these thoughts on paper). It's OK. Things are right.**

**Now, you've spent long enough reading. Let's talk while we get to that Chinese food. Love to and thanks for each of you, Dad.**

We talked for two hours. There were tears; there was some laughter. There was the question of how to advise my parents. Our children came up with the best answer: let's all do it together.

Before doing so, Mary Ann and I were to meet with Dr. Singleton and Dr. Bill Robinson. Dr. Robinson is the able Chief Oncologist at University Hospital. That meeting brought no better news than the previous one. Dr. Robinson said that I have a primary hepatoma in the liver, which is essentially incurable. The usual survival time is only a few months. I asked him to survey the country and to find any institution where experimental or innovative work on this problem is being done, and to his credit he did so, most professionally. But that did not come until later.

We returned home, collected the children and went to my parents to tell them the news and to invite them to spend the evening at our home because I knew it would be a shock for both of them. Again, there were tears, laughter and then that fierce determination which seems to be a part of the family. I advised my brothers and a few close friends and we survived the weekend.

The following Monday, I began a major trial of a Storage Technology case, involving a dispute of more than $100 million. I decided the best defense was a good offense and, as much as possible, we went about business as usual. However, the press had other thoughts. Reporters from both Denver daily papers, all of the Denver television stations, and assorted radio reporters got wind of my illness. I suggested that this was not terribly newsworthy, but they reminded me that the First Amendment gave them the right to make that decision, not me. As a result, there were stories in each paper, broadcasts on all four television channels and radio announcements. I told the reporters, "After a decade in politics, what's a little cancer in the belly?"

The result of the media coverage was a flood of hundreds of letters and calls from well-wishers, and it became apparent to me then that cancer is somehow a taboo subject, even though it affects one out of four people in this country and virtually every family has been or will be touched by it. It also became clear to me that the subject of death and dying, which is as much an inevitable life process as being born, is an equally taboo subject. I decided that, after the Storage Tech trial, I would try to do something about it.

We finished the trial and won the case. Dr. Robinson determined that the most advanced experimental work for this particular ailment was being done by Dr. Stanley Order at Johns Hopkins Hospital in Baltimore, Maryland. When we talked later in the week with Drs. Robinson and Singleton, Dr. Robinson had already made reservations for us to begin treatment the following Monday, December 17, at Johns Hopkins. Dr. Order has treated 200 people with this ailment, and while most treatments involving my condition have not been successful, he has enjoyed a higher success rate than anyone else in the nation. Beyond that, I liked both him and his approach. Between December 17 and December 28 I underwent 12 sessions of radiation and chemotherapy, finding time in between to fly back to Denver for a memorable Christmas. Further treatments were scheduled for January and later.

In addition to all of the concern and love from friends and well-wishers, groups of friends and acquaintances made Christmas caroling calls on us and bought us a VCR recorder and television set. Our previous television set was purchased during halftime of a football game some years before. I had, the previous summer, inadvertently squirted it with a hose, and for many months the color had run out of the set. It was a welcome and generous gift.

More than that, our good friend Jean Galloway realized that

what would be most helpful to me would be doing something on this whole subject of cancer, dying and hope.

We organized what may be the most comprehensive cancer awareness campaign in the history of the country, for which I agreed to serve as honorary chairman. Our goal is to involve 20,000 people in the greater Denver area, with a massive kick-off in the spring. In the meantime, the necessary media interviews, spot announcements and organization are being put in place. It is yet another campaign, but in this one there should be no losers. If we can make a dent on the public awareness and seriousness of this problem, it will have been a major contribution. No matter what happens, this experience has brought a new view of life's priorities, philosophy and quality, and the duty to one's fellow man. In the long run, it is true that it is the quality and not the quantity which counts. But all things considered, I'd rather be in Denver.

*Dale Tooley completed his book in February, 1985, and wrote of it to a friend:*

*"I have been at work on this project for more than a year and a half, and have revised it repeatedly, to the point where I am now fully satisfied with it."*

*He died on April 1, 1985.*

## ACKNOWLEDGEMENTS

| | |
|---|---|
| Editing: | Robert L. Tonsing |
| Recollections: | Jack W. Tooley<br>Thomas G. Brown<br>Hugh J. McClearn<br>Richard E. Young<br>Velma Andrews<br>Norman S. Early, Jr.<br>Jean Galloway<br>Justice O. Otto Moore |
| Photos: | Jody Strogoff/Colorado Statesman<br>Dick Burnell/Photo Associates<br>Duane Howell/The Denver Post<br>Jose Lopez, Mel Schieltz, John Gordon, Frank Murray and Steve Groer/ Rocky Mountain News<br>DeCroce Studio |
| Design: | Cheryl Meyer/Lafayette Studios |
| Typesetting: | Beckset Typesetting & Graphics |
| Printing: | Cottrell Printing Co. |
| Legal Counsel: | Ethan A. Jacobson |